LOUDER THAN WORDS

ALSO BY TODD HENRY

The Accidental Creative

Die Empty

LOUDER THAN WORDS

HARNESS THE POWER
OF YOUR AUTHENTIC VOICE

TODD HENRY

Portfolio / Penguin

PORTFOLIO / PENGUIN
An imprint of Penguin Random House LLC
375 Hudson Street
New York, New York 10014
penguin.com

ISBN 978-1-59184-752-6

Printed in the United States of America
1 3 5 7 9 10 8 6 4 2

Set in Adobe Jenson Pro
Designed by Spring Hoteling

For Rachel

CONTENTS

CONTENTS

PART 2
The Voice Engine

Chapter 4
Identity: Who Are You?

Chapter 5
Vision: Where Are You Going?

Chapter 6
Mastery: How Will You Get There?

PART 3
Everyday Application

Chapter 7
Everyday Practices for Developing Your Voice

Chapter 8
Developing Your Team's Voice

Chapter 9
Up the Curve

LOUDER THAN WORDS

Introduction

> When people don't express themselves, they die one
> piece at a time.
>
> —Laurie Halse Anderson, *Speak*

Your work tells tales. It speaks about you, your values, your hopes, your ambitions, and ultimately what you deem worthy of your energy and attention. It reveals, intentionally or not, what you really think about the world around you. Ultimately, your body of work—which is any place you create value, whether through your job, your relationships, or any other way you spend your time and energy—is a standing testament to your existence on this speck of rock orbiting the sun.

Here's a question worth pondering: While your work speaks about you, does it really speak *for* you? Does it represent you well? Does it reflect the authentic you? (Or, in your busyness, have you even recently considered who the authentic you might be?) The key to making your work resonate is to uncover, develop, and then bravely use your authentic voice.

What does this mean? When you are pouring yourself into your work and bringing your unique perspective and skills to the table, then you are adding value that only you are capable of contributing. However, many people operate in "default mode," and they ignore their hunches, their deeper intuition, and their unique vision, and instead settle into the fold. Over time, they become more of a reflection of everyone around them—or a faded photocopy of a photocopy—than an original source of ideas, energy, and life. Instead of doing the difficult work necessary to weave their influences together into something fresh and original, they settle for recycling the scraps in exchange for a quick return on their effort. In the end, they fall short of making a unique contribution that's reflective of what they truly care about, and because of a lack of individuality and passion, their work is less likely to resonate with their audience.

However, brilliant contributors commit to the process of developing an authentic voice through trial and error, by paying attention to how they respond to the work of peers, heroes, and even their antagonists, by playing with ideas, by cultivating a sharp vision for their work, and ultimately by honing their skills so that they have the ability to bring that vision to the world. If you examine the most contributive, impactful, and ultimately influential people throughout history, the one thing that clearly sets them apart is their unique voice. They had developed a personal expression that distanced them from their peers and put them in a field of their own. Their body of work speaks loudly about who they are and what they value. Louder, even, than their words.

Whether you are a writer, a consultant, an entrepreneur, an engineer, a manager, or an artist, developing your authentic voice should be a top priority if you are serious about crafting a body of work that will stand the test of time. Work, then, becomes about more than checking off tasks and pushing through projects. Instead, it is a means to carve a place in the world and create value that lasts. It becomes a means of genuine expression and a standing testament to your efforts.

WHAT IS VOICE?

For the purposes of this book, I'll define voice as the expression (idea) you make through a medium (platform) in order to achieve a desired outcome (impact). Whether you are creating a form of art, such as music or painting, or crafting a marketing message to reinforce your brand equity, your objectives will be accomplished by leveraging an expression through a medium, and the more resonant your message is with your audience, the more likely you will achieve your desired impact. Taken together, your collective body of work, as communicated through your voice, represents you, your style, your values, and your intentions.

Truly effective voices resound, meaning that others eventually become carriers of your expression. Ideally, your work will reach far beyond your immediate sphere of influence. However, crafting work that resounds isn't as simple as coming up with a viral meme or a catchy turn of phrase. While these tactics achieve short-term attention, a moment in the spotlight often fails to achieve lasting impact. This is why so many attention-grabbing television commercials never achieve long-term results for their brands. (A quick glance at post–Super Bowl audience survey results reveals that companies have paid millions of dollars for ads that as few as 35 percent of viewers associated afterward with their brand. Worse, a high percentage of viewers attributed them to their competitors. Perhaps the ads were memorable, but the company's voice wasn't distinguished enough from that of the competition to matter.) To resound means that your work connects deeply in some way with your audience, and that they in turn feel a connection to your work that's strong enough to compel them to respond, whether by sharing your work with others or by being mobilized to act in some way. The goal of developing an authentic voice isn't self-gratification, it's cultivating a greater ability to mobilize others toward a goal or objective, and in so doing achieve the impact you desire.

Those who are brave enough to dedicate themselves to the effort of discovering their authentic voice are impervious to the temporary cultural noise. Their work is founded upon a deep knowledge of who they are, what they want, and how they plan to achieve it. They have firm footing because they have rifled through the debris and uncovered bedrock. They have learned how to craft their work so that it represents their true selves and resonates with their audience.

HOW TO READ THIS BOOK

Louder Than Words is divided into three sections. The first section addresses the reason many people struggle to develop their voice, and the distinct phases that artists, entrepreneurs, writers, and others have passed through on their journey. The second section addresses what I refer to as the Voice Engine, or the mechanism that allows you to identify, develop, and use your voice to achieve impact. You will learn about the importance of Identity as a driving force for your work, Vision for defining the impact you want, and Mastery as a means of getting your ideas into the world more effectively. The final section offers more practical day-to-day advice for implementing your voice in the course of teamwork, as a leader, and as you plan and shape your work over the long term.

My goal is not to simply inspire you with a new approach to finding your voice but to inspire you to act differently as you shape your work. Though there will be a lot of reflective exercises, this book is written for people who are already moving, and are looking for signposts to help them get even better. This is a book for doers.

I hope to inspire you to seek an authentic voice, but you will see true growth only when you take action. There is no shortcut. In fact, as you develop your voice, you may often feel like you're failing even when you are on the verge of your greatest success. You will find yourself only if you are willing to first lose yourself in the process. It is the commitment to growth that matters, and small actions over time yield big results. As Don Baptiste, head of Bloomberg Government, told me in an interview, "You discover your voice by exercising it and getting in the mix. You might be surprised at what you find."

Don't project (and protect) an image of who you think you ought to be while abandoning your authentic self. Commit to the pursuit of brilliant work, even when immediate results are not guaranteed. As you'll soon see, this will require some self-excavation, and a lot of strategic experimentation. However, as with many things, it's your courage and willingness to engage in the journey that defines you. We need you to be brave, and to be yourself. We need you to develop your authentic voice, and to put it in the mix.

PART 1

The Journey of Developing Your Voice

Chapter 1

The Art of Resonance

Masterpieces are not single and solitary births; they are the outcome of many years of thinking in common, of thinking by the body of the people, so that the experience of the mass is behind the single voice.

—Virginia Woolf

Principle: To cultivate an authentic voice you must develop its three elements—Identity, Vision, and Mastery.

Have you ever heard yourself speaking or singing on a recording? I still remember the first time this happened to me, and when I played back the tape (yes, this was in the dark ages of analog recording), I couldn't believe how much different I sounded than what I'd expected. So much so, in fact, that it was almost as if I was hearing an entirely different person. (To my chagrin, I sounded less like a velvety Elvis Presley and more like a sad Pee-wee Herman.) Because of the resonance created in my skull by my vocal cords, I heard my own voice much differently than the recording revealed. This is the reason many people hate hearing the sound of their own, recorded voice. It sounds eerily foreign to them. (Do I really sound like that?)

I believe this same dynamic plays out with many people's metaphorical voice, though without the luxury of a playback button for immediate feedback. They are unaware of how their words and actions are collectively communicating to others. Worse, this lack of awareness may mean that they go about their lives and work behaving in a way that is inconsistent with who they really are, and perhaps even deeply disconnected from their true passions and ambitions. They project who they think they *should* be, and ignore the deeper signals about who they really *are*. Thus, they fail to infuse their authentic self into their work, and it fails to resonate deeply with others.

This is why I believe the most important work you will ever do is the work necessary to develop an authentic voice. I hope throughout this book to make the argument that your voice is both your single greatest possession and the most critical asset you share with the world. It is both the animating force for your best work and also the reason it gets noticed. And in the end, it is the source of both meaning and purpose in your work, and also the most likely generator of any success you experience.

By "authentic" I mean that your voice is sourced in the interplay of your unique passions, skills, and experiences. Contrary to how the word is often used today, this isn't necessarily about full transparency. Instead, it's about coming to a clear understanding of what you care about, then finding a way to infuse your work with the best of who you are so that it resonates in a unique way with your audience.

Your authentic voice is the expression of your compelling "why." It defines the space that you are wired to occupy, and the unique value you are capable of contributing, which means that if you don't use it, then that contribution is unlikely to ever be seen. Unfortunately, some of the myths about how an authentic voice is developed can be counterproductive. For example, advice such as "Just follow your gut" or "Do what you love and everything will work out" sounds exciting, but often fails to help you achieve lasting results and impact. As you'll see in the coming pages, developing your voice is not just about what you care about, it's also about how your passions intersect with what others care about. It's not only about what you say or do, it's about how your work is received.

The degree to which you develop and use your authentic voice in the course of your work will often determine whether or not you feel invested, effective, and even recognized in the ways that matter personally. (On the other hand, it's possible to be recognized for your work in ways that don't matter to you and find that it feels like hollow praise. If you are not making personally meaningful progress in your work, no amount of success in the eyes of others is likely to fill the void.)

In etymological terms, our word *voice* is closely tied to the root of the word *vocation*, which is the term many people use as a substitute for the word job. However, I find it helpful to draw a sharp distinction between the words *occupation* and *vocation*. Your occupation is how you make a living, or at least what you spend most of your day doing. Your vocation, on the other hand, is the activity or expression you are naturally drawn to when given latitude over how to spend your focus, assets, time, and energy. It's the sort of work that you feel compelled to do even when no one is paying attention. The active form of your vocation, and the way it's experienced by others, is your voice.

Your occupation is simply a platform. It's the arena in which you are given a chance to create an impact. For example, your job ideally allows you the opportunity to influence and change the world around you, even if it's in a small way. Your vocation, on the other hand, is the expression that you make *through* your platform. It's the unique value you add, and your authentic response to your environment. Your vocation cannot be fully contained by your occupation. It finds expression in all areas of your life.

Have you ever felt especially alive at the end of a meeting, task, or project? Maybe it's because something went really well, and you know that it simply wouldn't have happened without your efforts. It's more than just the rush of relief for having checked something off your list; it's that the value of your unique perspective and skills has been affirmed and that you've done something no one else could have. You experienced the thrill of operating in your "sweet spot." In these circumstances, your vocation, or calling, has found expression through your occupation. This is often when we feel most alive and contributive in our work. However, for many people, it's difficult to bridge the steep gap between who they are and what they do each day. Instead of heeding their intuition and taking risks with their work, they do what is expected, and play it safe by taking the tried-and-true route, trying not to stand out. As a result, their impact is limited, and they experience less of the joy that comes from pouring their unique and authentic self into their work.

Unfortunately, many people spend the bulk of their time trying to figure out how to grow their platform (their sphere of influence), but neglect the much more critical process of developing their voice. As a result, while they may grow the level of awareness for their work, their impact stalls over time because it is not rooted in something of substance. Your voice is the fuel that sustains your pace, and without it you will eventually lose steam. You cannot succeed through platform alone, at least not in the ways that matter.

THE VOICE ENGINE

To develop your authentic voice, you must cultivate three things: a strong sense of identity, which means doing work that is rooted in something substantive and personally meaningful; a consonant vision for your work, meaning a sense of the ultimate impact you want to have; and mastery of your skills and platform.

A strong, authentic, compelling voice is the expression of identity, guided by vision, and achieved through mastery. These three work together as a part of the lifelong process of growth and discovery. Developing your authentic voice is the result of lifelong layers of learning, experimentation, and failure. While it's possible to piece it all together over time through trial and error, I want to help you accelerate the process by building practices around each of these three core drivers.

Identity is primarily defined by the question "Who are you?" If I informally ask you that question, there are a number of ways you could respond. You could tell me about your childhood experiences, your job, your hobbies, your political views, or any number of other defining characteristics. However you respond, it would be a story about how you perceive yourself and your place in the world. In fact, your sense of identity is a collection of these stories. Whether the stories are true or false is somewhat irrelevant, because it's whether or not you believe them that defines how you behave. Regardless of what you profess to believe, your actions reveal the truth. When you act in a manner that's inconsistent with your true aptitudes and passions, it can create frustration, and over time can lead to a sense that you're not living up to your creative potential.

Thus, self-knowledge is a critical ingredient of identity, because when it is lacking you are more likely to compromise your true thoughts and beliefs. This is especially true when you are under pressure to deliver results. You must have a rooted understanding of why your work matters to you, what makes it unique, and why you believe it should also matter to others. I can often tell when someone is having an identity crisis, because they will communicate in one of two ways: broadly so as not to offend anyone, or so specifically and reactively (in order to appear confident) that they self-contradict when the winds of public opinion grow unfavorable to their previous stance. Your work must be rooted in something of substance so that you don't blow with the winds of change or challenge. As you'll see in the coming pages, thoughtful action is the best form of self-discovery.

The second part of the Voice Engine is vision, which is primarily defined by the question "Where are you going?" If you set out to build a bridge between two points on a river, you'd better first determine (a) the purpose of the bridge and the kinds of vehicles that will be crossing it, (b) whether you have sufficient resources and materials to complete the project, and (c) whether or not a bridge is even the right solution to the problem of crossing the river. To apply this metaphor to your work, it's important that you are able to articulate the kind of effect you wish to have, and how you want the world to be different through your efforts. You should at least have a sense of how you wish to connect with an intended audience, and how you plan to impact them. Though you don't want to become paralyzed with inaction out of fear of getting it wrong, your vision provides you with a set of guiding principles to help you stay aligned and measure your progress.

Many people falsely believe that brilliant contributors just follow their whims and let their "gut" decide from moment to moment where their work will lead them, but this is largely untrue. Though they rarely have all of their steps mapped out, the majority of the great creators and teams I've encountered at least have some sense of where their work is leading and the ultimate impact they want to have. They have a "north pole" toward which to navigate, even if only in a general sense. This vision is what guides their efforts as they continue to refine and develop their voice.

The final piece of the Voice Engine is mastery, which is defined by the question "How will you get there?" As you sharpen your skills, you have more tools in your toolbox and give yourself more options for expression. It's obvious that people who sharpen their skills and hone their instincts are far better positioned to create value, but in the midst of the daily fray we often forget to devote energy to personal skill and platform development. Brilliant contributors know that an opportunity exists only if they are able to recognize it and take advantage of it. In order to use your voice in ways that matter, you have to hone your skills so that you are prepared to jump on opportunities as they emerge. Mastery is also about honing your instincts and engaging in daily practice so that you develop the kinds of perceptions necessary to make intuitive leaps. No matter how skilled you are, if you don't have an outlet for that expertise, you will not succeed.

So your answers to these three questions, "Who are you?" "Where are you going?" and "How will you get there?" give you a map for developing your authentic voice. Your sense of identity leads you to a compelling vision, which then illuminates the skills and platform you need to master in order to succeed.

When all three of these elements are working together, they create a virtuous cycle of growth and effectiveness. You engage in self-discovery through action, refine your vision, and master new skills along the way. However, when one or more of the drivers of the Voice Engine are lacking, there is likely to be an outage in your ability to resonate with your audience.

IDENTITY + VISION — MASTERY = NOT CREDIBLE

You can have a clear sense of identity, and you can be guided by a compelling vision, but if you haven't developed the skills necessary to share your work effectively, then it will fall short. You can yell louder than everyone else, but you will still achieve little lasting impact. This is often the situation early in your career, as you are gaining your footing but still lack the skills necessary to accomplish your vision. You lack credibility, because your skills and platform for influence don't measure up to your ambition.

IDENTITY + MASTERY — VISION = NOT CLEAR

Your audience craves clarity, and will seek out work by those who know where they are headed. Without a vision for your work you are like a ship at sea, unable to weather the storms of contrary opinions or challenges to your point of view. Your work may waffle and ramble to the point of confusion, and even early fans of your work will eventually lose hope and abandon you if they can't discern where you are leading them. Your vision is the compass that keeps you on the right bearing even while "making it up as you go."

MASTERY + VISION — IDENTITY = NOT CALLED

Without an identity-infused voice, your body of work will ultimately be hollow. Your audience is likely to discount you if your work feels inauthentic. This often happens when someone is chasing trends rather than aiming for impact. (Consider the trend of rapidly spreading but ultimately shallow list-based blog posts, or attention-grabbing headlines that may garner someone's focus for a short period but will not ultimately lead to any kind of significant impact other than momentary entertainment.) This is not to imply that all clever attempts to gain attention for your work are misplaced, but your body of work will be inconsistent if it's not rooted in something that matters to you.

IDENTITY + VISION + MASTERY = COMPELLING

When all the parts of the engine are working together, they fuel the discovery and use of your authentic voice. A greater sense of identity leads to a refined vision, which provides motivation to continue to master new skills. Through this greater mastery, you achieve influence, which then ideally helps you better understand your place in the world, and leads to a deeper understanding of the value you want to create. The cycle continues to repeat over and over throughout your life.

As you examine the above equations, which do you think most accurately describes you at the present time? Which of the three drivers are you best at, and weakest at? It's easy to get out of balance, as you deal with the pressures of work, family, and other responsibilities. This is why it's important to have a set of grounding practices to help you continue growing. In the coming pages, you'll discover tools to help you hone and strengthen your sense of identity, your vision for your work, and your mastery over your platform for expression. In other words, to answer "who are you?" "where are you going?" and "how will you get there?"

CHECKPOINT

Each of the following chapters will include the following checkpoints to help you stay aligned and focused, assess where you are with regard to the three drivers of the Voice Engine, and help you consider potential next steps on your journey of growth and discovery.

Excavation: You must first get to the "bedrock," or the core and guiding concerns, influences, and experiences that make your perspective unique. Why should anyone care what you think? Why should anyone listen to what you have to say? What makes your ideas more valuable than the ideas of others?

Observation: To grow, you must play the role of scientist. Which forms of expression seem to have the most impact? Which seems to resonate most deeply with your audience, or with you personally? By noting these areas of impact you can improve your precision and authority.

Redirection: Knowledge without action is useless. You must take what you uncover about yourself and apply it in the course of your daily work. Over time, you will develop a unique style or form of expression that helps you convey your thoughts and ideas.

EXCAVATION

As you consider the three elements of the Voice Engine (Identity, Vision, Mastery), which do you think is your strongest link? Which do you feel is your weakest? Everyone has a need for continued growth in each of these three areas, but identifying which one you struggle with the most can help you determine how to focus your efforts in the near term.

OBSERVATION

Think of a time in your life when you succeeded in doing work that influenced others and achieved the results you desired. What made it especially effective? Can you describe some qualities that reflect why that work was especially resonant with your audience?

REDIRECTION

As you go about your work this week, remind yourself daily of those moments when you were especially impactful, and the qualities that made your work resonant. As a starting point, try to infuse your work this week with more of those same qualities. (As we progress into later chapters, you'll learn some specific tools to help you do so.)

Chapter 2

The Hurdles

For us moderns, perhaps, fear of being ridiculous in our own eyes is the greatest shame.

—Dorothee Soelle, *Death by Bread Alone*

Principle: To develop your authentic voice you must overcome the forces that keep you in a place of conformity and comfort.

Imagine yourself standing on the edge of a canyon, preparing to hike to the other side. Below you can see trees, the river flowing through the canyon, and the beauty of the landscape surrounding it. From your privileged position you can see the entirety of the terrain, the path down and back up the other wall of the chasm, and the ending point of your journey. It seems so simple, and you have plenty of energy for the hike. You're excited about the possibility of reaching the other side, and you set out at an aggressive pace. However, as you descend into the canyon, you become less certain of your position. The tall trees make it difficult to navigate, and the steepness of the decline is taking a toll on your knees. You are rapidly losing energy, and you know that sundown is coming in just a few hours. Given the wildlife known to prowl the area, you do not want to be caught in the canyon at night.

In the midst of your hike, you can no longer see the end objective. The path that was so clear at the top is now difficult to discern. You know you're still headed generally in the right direction, but this trek has proven to be much more challenging than it appeared from your launching point. After much effort and muddling, you spot your target destination through a clearing in the treetops, and below it an entry point back to the path. You navigate toward it, but you suddenly realize that you now have a long, uphill climb in order to complete your hike by sundown, and your legs are starting to give. However, this is where your training kicks in, and before long you get your second wind. Up you climb, eyes on the destination, with the path now obvious and open, but knowing that you have to hustle in order to make it by dark. Finally, just before the sun slips over the horizon, you step up onto the ledge of the opposite side. As you turn around and glance back, you have a newfound respect for the canyon that seemed so simple and traversable at the outset.

The journey through the canyon is similar to how every creative endeavor takes shape. Artist and illustrator Lisa Congdon once shared with me a bit of advice she received from an art teacher who had greatly impacted her life. He told her that every creative project, regardless of what kind, has a U shape. You begin the project with a clear plan and great enthusiasm, but as you engage in the work your natural energy for the project begins to fade. Things that once seemed so simple when you were at the top of the curve are now more complex, muddy, and unclear. What once appeared clearly in your mind is no longer so straightforward. This is the point where many people give up.

However, if you stick with the project through the deepest part of the U, your passion begins to swell again, patterns form, you eventually find the path, and your energy level returns, perhaps even in greater measure. When this happens, the resulting work is far better than ever seemed possible in the valley of despair.

Every creative project—writing a book, starting a business, or building a blog—follows this same U shape. If you rely solely on your emotions to guide you, it's likely you'll give up just as you're on the uptick again. Instead, you must be guided by a larger vision for your work, and keep the end goal in sight, even when it's obscured by complication and frustration.

The process of developing your voice is the process of navigating a series of U shapes. There will be peaks upon which everything seems so clear and your work is so on target that you want to share it with everyone you meet, and there will be valleys in which you question why you're even trying. It's all part of the process, and it's never ending. However, the key is to remain focused on your vision and embrace the journey. As famed sculptor Auguste Rodin remarked, "Nothing is a waste of time if you use the experience wisely." The peaks, the valleys, and the struggles in between are all useful in pointing you toward the brilliance that's being called out of you. Nothing is wasted.

THE HURDLES YOU MUST JUMP

Unfortunately, many people experience the struggles at the bottom of the canyon and misinterpret them as a sign that they are in the wrong place. They believe that if they were truly on the right path, everything would fall into place easily. This narrative causes a great many people to stop short of discovering the work that could really fulfill them. I shudder to think of how much brilliant work was abandoned simply because of a lack of certainty.

You will rarely be certain you are moving in the right direction, especially when you are headed into uncharted creative territory. Uncertainty causes many people to hover close to the middle, or squarely in their comfort zone, and to avoid anything that might expose them to risk. However, the pursuit of voice is about not only recognizing the potential of risk but embracing it as an essential part of growth. Moves that appear the least risky in the short term are often the most risky in the long term, because they keep you among the huddled masses of those who are doing expected, mediocre work. The unspoken truth is that very few people ever become comfortable with risk, but brilliant contributors recognize that without measured risk in your life you will not grow.

Over time, this daily uncertainty and the lack of guaranteed results can cause our passion to wane, squelch our ambition, or, worse, cause us to settle into a pattern of producing work that we know does not reflect the true power of our authentic voice. The better we understand the hurdles that stand in our way, the better equipped we will be to tap into the practices that will aid us in countermanding them.

HURDLE #1: PARALYSIS DUE TO FEAR

Remember the monster that lived in your closet or under your bed when you were a child? Almost everyone I've talked to had some variation of this. I remember being so paralyzed at night that I would refuse to get out of bed even for the most urgent of matters (ahem) and would wait instead until daybreak, sometimes with disastrous results. I just knew that the moment my feet hit the floor I would be monster food. Was this a rational fear? Of course not! If you'd asked me during the daytime I'd probably have told you it was silly. But was it very real in the moment, when the house was dark and the wind was whipping outside my window? Definitely.

In the 2004 M. Night Shyamalan movie *The Village*, a group of villagers is living together in a clearing in the woods. They are told from birth not to venture into the woods because there are monsters —"those we don't speak of"—who agreed not to enter the village as long as the villagers stay out of their territory. It turns out (spoiler alert) that this story was simply a ruse to keep the villagers under control.

These monster stories are not much different from the stories we tell today to keep one another in check. Our culture loves inventing "those we don't speak of" to create a sense of relative peace and stability. "Just stay where you are, keep your head down, don't make waves, and it's all going to work out fine." After all, if you start taking risks you're just asking for trouble. There are all sorts of monsters waiting for you out there, in the dark and the uncertainty. While there are definitely very real risks involved in pursuing a unique voice and doing remarkable work, many of the fears that paralyze us and prevent us from acting are not much different from that imagined monster under our bed. They are overinflated ("I will be a laughing-stock," or "I'll be ruined"), often irrational, and in no way as harmful or likely as we imagine, yet they still stop us from action. In these moments of paralysis, our need for conformity trumps our desire for contribution.

There are a lot of practical reasons why our ancestors craved this kind of communal conformity. Conformity through shared practices and beliefs ensured the highest degree of protection against outsiders, and a strong sense of borrowed identity. Pooling together meant leveraging the strengths of the whole, even though it was at the expense of individuality. Thus, to be an outcast was—in many cases—a death sentence, because it exposed you to the dangers of the world without the collective protection of your community.

Even though being an outcast is no longer deadly in the same way, the residual desire to conform still inhibits many people today. Though they want to be received by others for who they truly are, they are willing to sacrifice their deeper sense of identity and compromise their vision in order to fit in. In a culture that wants to categorize everything, it's tough to be seen as "different" or as "an outlier." Thus, they subvert their identity in order to adopt the identity of their chosen group.

It's easy to see this dynamic at play with teenagers as they try on various identities in order to see which ones fit. In some cases, they are practicing conformity through nonconformity as they latch on to others and form cliques. It's a way of playing with identity and voice within the relative safety of community, but it is also frequently driven by a fear of not fitting in somewhere. As you'll see in the next chapter, experimentation and association are natural parts of developing your own voice, but for some the identity morphing never ends. Beneath the fear of pursuing an authentic voice is often a deeper fear that they might not be all that unique, or that they may not like what they find. This happens in organizational life as well, when a cult of personality develops around an especially charismatic leader, and over time you begin to see people on the team emulating the same mannerisms, language, or habits as the leader. However, mindless cohesion can be the kiss of death for any creative team, because it means compromising the brilliance of individuals for the sake of conformity and comfort.

At its heart, the fear of not fitting in is a fear of rejection, often stemming from the concern that poor performance will mean (a) alienation from the group, (b) a degradation of self-worth or self-perception, and (c) possible loss of livelihood. Most of us have experienced this fear, whether when asked to offer our opinion in a meeting, to deliver a proposal for a new direction for a project, or when simply considering whether or not to share some work we've been toiling away at in private. We may have strong convictions in private, but the moment we are asked to share them publicly, we begin to sift our thoughts through filter after filter to determine the risk associated with being completely honest. On our worst days, we may clam up and parrot back something that feels safe (in the moment). On our best days, we are brave enough to stand against the tide of public opinion, even knowing the potential cost.

If you want to do unique, contributive work, and develop your voice, you must have the courage to offend. You must recognize that there will be some people who just don't get it, and muster the courage to keep moving forward anyway. You must be willing to act on your intuitive hunches.

Question: Are you afraid to offend people with your work? If so, why?

After an early performance at the Grand Ole Opry, an industry insider told Elvis Presley that he would be better off returning to his job in Memphis as a truck driver. In a 2010 *Vanity Fair* article, photographer Al Wertheimer described what it was like to follow the King around during his heyday as a pioneer of rock and roll. "He dared to move," says Wertheimer. "Singers just did not move onstage in those days. You stood there like Frank Sinatra or Perry Como, and you sang from the waist up. Elvis broke all the rules. He moved his hips. He charged the microphone. He was introducing something that was just not acceptable to grown-ups and the more conservative groups. I have the William Morris guys getting him into a corner, and they're giving him advice: 'Now, Elvis, look, you get up there, you sing your song, but don't move too much.' Elvis dutifully listened. He wouldn't argue with them. But once he got onstage he did what he wanted." What made Elvis Presley unique was that he followed his intuition about what would connect with his audience, even when all the norms of the time told him otherwise. He sensed that audiences were ready for a fusion of R&B with gospel, and a mashup of squeaky-clean looks with a raucous performance previously seen only in smoky, less-than-reputable venues. By following his intuition, accepting the potential of rejection, and embracing risk, trial, and error, he crafted a unique style of performance that became part of his signature voice.

There are many other examples of creative work that are now considered brilliant and iconic, but were at first panned by critics. F. Scott Fitzgerald's *The Great Gatsby*, widely hailed as one of the greatest books of the twentieth century, was once rejected by a publishing executive who said, "You'd have a decent book if you'd get rid of that Gatsby character." In 1962, Decca recording executive Dick Rowe reportedly told Brian Epstein, manager of The Beatles, "We don't like their sound. Groups of guitars are on the way out," in his now infamous rejection of the Fab Four. The more boldly you choose a path for your work, the more rejection you will face from those who don't immediately understand it.

Unfortunately, many people are unwilling to risk this kind of critique. The net result is that they stay close to the middle, unwilling to take the risks necessary to develop an authentic voice, and thus go unnoticed. They fail to do the very things they know would lead to brilliant work.

When I was younger, I was psychologically paralyzed by the fear of rejection. Shortly out of college I had a job with an eyewear company that required me to call optometrists who were delinquent on their rent and remind them that their payment was past due. (As you can imagine, this made me very popular.) More than once I dialed every digit of the phone number except the last one, then paused while trying to muster up the courage to complete the task. Even though I was clearly in the power seat in the situation—I imagine the doctors were far more nervous about hearing from me than I was about calling them—I was still terrified at the thought that I was delivering unwelcome news. In some distorted way, my personal identity had become intertwined with the job, so in my mind a rejection of the news I bore equaled some kind of personal rejection. I've encountered many creative professionals who bear a similar kind of fear of rejection. Their work is an extension of themselves, and any rejection of the work is a rejection of their very value as a person. However, this limiting narrative often curbs their willingness to pursue their authentic voice.

Question: Do you perceive a rejection of your work as a rejection of your worth?

In 2013, I heard a man named Jia Jiang give an account of his personal struggle with the fear of rejection. Early in life, Jiang had big dreams of entrepreneurship and financial success. Inspired by the story of Bill Gates, he once wrote a letter to his family informing them that he would start a company that by age twenty-five he would grow into the largest company in the world. (Additionally, he added that his company would someday acquire Microsoft.) Armed with youthful ambition, Jiang entered the workforce out of college, but life—as it tends to do—incrementally complicated his journey toward world domination. He took a good job, which led to promotions and raises, a marriage, and a child. However, something didn't quite sit right with him, and deep down he felt that he had compromised his true vision for where his body of work should be headed.

Jiang communicated his concern to his wife. He told her that he'd come to the realization that if he didn't take action on his dreams, he would someday die of regret. They concocted a plan in which he would quit his job and spend six months attempting to gain traction on his own. They decided that at the end of the six months, if there was no visible sign of progress, he would look for another job.

About four months into the experiment, it seemed as if things were turning for the better. Jiang had a lead on an investment opportunity that he believed he would be able to leverage into a sustainable venture for his family. It seemed as if his risk might actually pan out. However, one evening Jiang received a call with crushing news. The deal, he discovered, was off. The news hit him harder than he'd expected. Somehow, the rejection of the deal had become internalized as a personal rejection—as a measure of his personal worth—and it was quite painful. Dejected, Jiang resolved that perhaps he had been foolhardy to leave a perfectly stable job in order to start again from scratch.

Only four and a half months into the venture, Jiang told his wife that perhaps his ambition to start a business wasn't meant to be after all. "She was like a quarterback," he said. "She grabbed my face mask, stood toe to toe with me, and said, 'I gave you six months, not four! Now go make it work!'"

It was about this time that Jiang stumbled across something called rejection therapy. Jiang thought that perhaps his fear of rejection was inhibiting his efforts to build a business, so he decided to intentionally pursue rejection in order to prove to himself that it's not the end of the world. However, he knew that without some measure of accountability, he might not follow through, so he decided to document his experiment through a project he called "100 Days of Rejection." He captured video of himself approaching complete strangers and making audacious requests along with their responses. At first, his requests were fairly simple, like knocking on a door and asking to play soccer in someone's backyard. Over time, however, Jiang became more bold. He once flagged down a police officer and asked to drive his patrol car. At an airport, he asked the pilot of a single-engine plane if he could take it for a spin.

"The funny thing is," Jiang reflected of his experience, "people said yes!" While flying over cornfields and high over the plains, he considered how many experiences he'd missed out on, simply because he didn't ask. In perhaps his most recognized act of rejection seeking,

Jiang visited a Krispy Kreme doughnut shop and asked whether they could prepare him something special—a doughnut comprised of six interconnected doughnuts, frosted to look like the Olympic rings. Though caught off guard, the cashier replied, "When would you need it?" to which Jiang replied, "How about the next fifteen minutes?" A few minutes later, the worker emerged from the kitchen carrying Jiang's special-ordered doughnut. Additionally, she said that there would be no charge.

"I've come to learn that rejection is an opinion," Jiang said of his experience. He said that it's only when we allow it to become an objective statement about our self-worth that rejection holds any power over us.

This fear of rejection is precisely what prevents many people from taking risks with their work, choosing a unique path, and finding their authentic voice. However, once you recognize that rejection is simply an opinion, it frees you to follow your intuition and add unique value. You cannot allow the fear of rejection to silence you.

There isn't a single successful person I've encountered, including internationally esteemed business leaders, politicians, artists, and entrepreneurs, who hasn't at some point felt inadequate to the task. The key to making a contribution, and ultimately finding your voice, is often the simple willingness to act in the face of fear and uncertainty.

You have to let go of your fear of what you think you must be so that you can embrace the possibility of what you might be. It is deeply ingrained in the human condition to simultaneously crave recognition and camouflage. We want our unique abilities to show, but deep down we fear that we're really not so great. These two forces battle within us, and then paralyze us. As a result, we show enough of ourselves to differentiate us from the competition, but not so much as to isolate us. We follow the herd when it's expedient, but shun them when the stakes are low.

Of course, no one wants to behave this way. We all want to be brave, speak our mind, and do work that stands out, but the biological urge for conformity and perceived safety is strong. An idea inspires a surge of enthusiasm, and a fraction of a second later a stern internal voice of warning pulls you back to safe ground. Instead of taking small, calculated steps in the direction of your intuition, you stay silent or rationalize why the idea wasn't so great to begin with.

Question: Is fear of rejection causing you to self-edit or play it safe with your work?

HURDLE #2: FALSE OR LIMITING NARRATIVES

A false or limiting narrative can prevent people and organizations from taking action, and stop them from developing an authentic voice. Somehow a belief has become embedded, that belief has fossilized into an entrenched assumption, and that assumption is now limiting their scope of vision and preventing them from acting in a way that's true to who they really are.

Richard Hytner is the worldwide deputy chairman of advertising giant Saatchi & Saatchi. He told me that over the course of his career, he filled many kinds of leadership roles within companies, large and small, including the CEO role of publicly traded companies. Over time he has come to realize that his real strength is not in being the top person but in being a leader supporting the "number one." Hytner borrowed a term from the Italian Mafia to describe this kind of leader: consiglieri. The consiglieri is the counselor to the most powerful person in the organization. Though they are not in the ultimate position of accountability and authority, they are nonetheless an indispensable part of the effectiveness of an organization because they are able to provide a level of candor and perspective that is often lacking at the topmost levels.

However, Hytner says that it can be challenging to be the person best equipped to fill the consiglieri role, because it's not one that is typically celebrated in our culture. We celebrate the stories of the "top dog," or the person who climbs to the top of the mountain and stands victorious on the peak, not the person carrying the gear along the way. For this reason, a lot of people are hesitant to accept a path in which they fill the consiglieri role, even if that's the best forum in which they can pursue their authentic voice. There is a limiting narrative that causes many people to jump off the path of contribution, onto the one that is more likely to inspire others.

If you don't get to the bottom of these narratives, then you may struggle to develop your voice. You may instead find that you are living out someone else's story. There are two general categories of narratives that you must be aware of: personal narratives and collective narratives.

Personal narratives: No matter what you say, you will ultimately act out the narrative that you truly believe. These narratives become like scripts, or continuous messages that play in our head. Over time, they become embedded beliefs about who we are, our role in the world, and our capabilities and limitations. We tell ourselves stories in order to make it easier to cope with the possibility of failure, or to help us deal with the pressures of success, but we're smart enough to know they aren't true.

We often ignore the role that this "self-talk" plays in our daily work, but its effects can be massive. If you paid attention for only a few hours to the kinds of things running through your mind, you might be shocked.

One example of how these destructive narratives can paralyze even the best and brightest is a man named Joseph. He was struggling to get moving on a big project—one that could have tremendous implications for his career prospects and income over the next few years—and he needed help. No matter what he tried, and no matter how intentional he was about structuring his life to help him make progress, whenever he sat down to do the work he simply went blank. It was like he had nothing to give, even though he'd proven himself to be quite capable with several similar projects.

"I feel like I might be blowing it," he told me. "This is possibly the biggest opportunity I've ever had, and I also feel less motivated than I've ever been to work on it. I'm afraid that I'm hitting bottom right at the very moment I need to be peaking."

I knew what he meant, because I'd been there myself on multiple occasions. It's a terrible feeling, because when opportunity comes along you have to be prepared to capitalize at a moment's notice. Knowing that the opportunity is sitting in front of you, but the work isn't flowing, is a nightmare. However, I recalled something about Joe's recent history that I thought he might be overlooking.

I said, "Tell me about the last project you worked on that was similar in scope to this one."

His eyes locked with mine as if I'd just dealt a strong blow to his psyche. "Well, it didn't go so well." He explained that he'd felt really great about the work he did on the project, and when he turned it in he was excited about what it might mean for his career. However, the results were far less than impressive. Response to his work was underwhelming. In fact, compared with his expectations, it would be fair to say that it was a failure.

"Is it accurate to say," I inquired, speaking carefully, "that you were pretty disappointed with how the last project turned out?"

Again, the glare from Joseph. "Yes. There was a lot of disappointment."

"Why?"

A pause. "Well, I was very proud of my work. I thought it was some of the best I'd ever done. On top of that, it was a project I cared a lot about, so I was excited to see others' response to it, because I really felt it would be a career-defining thing."

"And?"

"It wasn't. There was some response, but it just didn't resonate the way I'd hoped. I guess I just thought that it would be my breakthrough, but instead it kind of flopped, which was frustrating after all of the intense work that went into it."

I could tell that Joseph's block wasn't really about a lack of ideas, or a lack of resources, but was instead due to a deep disappointment about the performance of his recent project. He was simply struggling to get motivated to pour himself into another project when the results of the other side of his effort were so uncertain. More than that, he'd grown disillusioned as he saw the work of others, which in a candid moment he admitted he deemed not nearly as good as his own, sail past his and receive wide recognition.

The narrative that was paralyzing Joseph went something like this: "Don't get your hopes up and put too much of yourself into this project. After all, you don't want to be disappointed again, which is the most likely outcome. It's not worth it."

At the heart of it, this lack of motivation stems from the same kind of disappointment that Joseph was dealing with. There was a narrative playing in his mind that told him to self-protect. When you've had a few disappointments in your career, a self-protection narrative starts to form and can prevent you from pouring yourself too fully into your work, which then causes a self-fulfilling prophecy when you underperform. It's often a downward spiral.

There is a bit of good news in the midst of all this. Once you identify these destructive narratives, you can begin to weed them out of your life and your organization. Even better, you can replace them with more productive and focused narratives that help you align with where you want to go.

Here's the thing about personal, limiting narratives: they often have an acute source. When there is a weight of authority behind the narrative—when it's introduced by a parent, a teacher, a manager, or someone you respect—it can modify your behavior in undesirable ways, and those behaviors can become self-reinforcing habits, or entrenched beliefs, and rob you of your ability to take meaningful and productive risks with your work. You obey the authoritative voices of others, even long after they are absent from your life. As ridiculous as it seems, I still occasionally feel the sting of my junior high football coach's words or a college professor's critique of my writing, but I've come to learn that I'm not the only one who struggles with voices from the past. I had one person approach me after a speech and tell me that she can still hear the chiding words of her first manager telling her that she wasn't cut out for her industry. Though it was now twenty years later, and she had more than proven her abilities, those words would still play in her mind whenever she faced potential failure in a project.

Question: Is there a limiting narrative that plays on a recurring loop in your head? If so, where do you think it came from?

In his 2004 book *Status Anxiety*, contemporary philosopher and author Alain de Botton argues that a unique challenge of living and working in community is our tendency to compare our accomplishments and relative standing with others in the community. When given discretion over the kind of work we do and the kind of value we create, we tend to compare that value in relative terms to others around us, and to draw conclusions about our social standing based upon our observations of relative rank, wealth, or social recognition. We seek, even if subconsciously, the stamp of approval of our peer group. We want to be noteworthy, or to stand out from the crowd. De Botton notes, "According to one influential wing of modern secular society, there are few more disreputable fates than to end up being 'like everyone else'—for 'everyone else' is a category that embraces the mediocre and the conformist, the boring and the suburban. The goal of all right-thinking people, so this argument goes, should be to distinguish themselves from the crowd and 'stand out' in whatever way their talents will allow."

However, this narrative that demands that we "stand out" can also have a paralyzing effect. We scan the horizon for approval, or mimic what we see being celebrated, and our work becomes hollow, lacking life or true depth of meaning. We settle for attention and sacrifice contribution and growth. Oddly, striving to make something unique in the eyes of others can cause us to lose connection with the one source of true uniqueness we have to offer—our authentic voice.

Question: Is a need to stand out causing you to do work that is inconsistent with who you believe yourself to be?

Collective narratives: Just like individuals can allow false narratives to erode their sense of mission and siphon out the best parts of their culture, organizations can also adopt narratives about their work that limit their ability to do their best each day. These are the stories we (unwittingly) tell ourselves about why an organization exists, and why we behave as we do. Often these narratives creep into a team over the course of many years and become so endemic that we can't even recognize them any longer. They are simply the air we breathe. (As Albert Einstein wrote in a 1936 essay, "What does a fish know about the water in which he swims all his life?") From the inside it's difficult to judge the veracity of these narratives, and over time they shape and limit our ability to pursue a unique and evolving team voice.

"That would never fly here."

"Dissent is a sign of mutiny."

"Just do whatever the client asks, no questions."

"We're capable of only midtier work."

What makes these group narratives so sinister is that they are often mindlessly passed down through generations of the organization. New hires are excited and full of hope, but over time they become jaded as they succumb to limiting narratives.

The thing about these narratives is that they can easily become so ingrained in our consciousness that they actually begin to seem like incontrovertible truth. They come guised as wisdom, because they are often sourced in the voices of authority figures from our past (like the well-meaning teacher, coach, or parent) or other authorities in our life who have an alternative agenda for us (like a manager or competitive peer). However, they are—in all ways—like lead weights connected to our heels. They will ultimately drag us to a halt.

Question: Is there a collective narrative that is stunting the growth or silencing the authentic voice of your team? What is it, and where do you think it came from?

You must deal with the false narratives in order to develop your authentic voice. In some form or fashion, we all battle a fear of insignificance and wrestle with the stigma of rejection. We are all, to some extent, afraid to act because we dread coming to the edge of our own ability. We'd rather live with the perception of invincibility than test our limits. Thus, instead of becoming the best flautist in the orchestra, we wish we were a violinist, and the violinist wishes that she were a conductor. Instead of being the right tackle on the football team, we wish to be the quarterback. We need to overcome this fear of insignificance and replace it with a mind-set of contribution. Everyone has a unique role to play, but that role is uncovered and developed over time through deliberate action and awareness.

HURDLE #3: INERTIA

For years, my work commute was twenty minutes by car. I would head out the door, coffee in hand, hop into the driver's seat, and pull out onto the road. Often, I would pull into the parking lot at work shocked that I'd arrived so quickly. It had seemed like only a few minutes, because I was strictly on autopilot. Because I'd driven that route so many times, I could do it without thinking, and my mind was often on my first meeting or a perplexing project I was trying to navigate. The only time I came out of my hypnosis was when someone veered into my lane or I noticed something unusual on a billboard.

In a similar way, many of us have set our lives (and work) to cruise control. We're just heading down the same path we've been on for years, navigating by instinct, and doing it all without really considering how things might be different.

Your authentic voice can be stunted by simple inertia, or staying for too long on the easiest, most familiar path. It's much easier to go with the flow than to be in a mode of continual redirection. It feels better to latch on to something that seems like a "sure bet," or to protect the ground you've already taken than to attempt to stake new ground. This is especially true once you've experienced a degree of success and recognition for a certain kind of work. Contrary to conventional wisdom, which says it's less risky to try new things once you're successful, the more successful you become, the more risky it can feel to try something new. The relative risk feels much higher because there is so much more to protect.

Many who are trapped by inertia lament that they feel stuck, whether by circumstances, by their organization, or by their own lack of ability. Often this feeling of "stuckness" is the result of their perception of the expectations of others. They escalate those expectations to the point that any kind of "out of bounds" action seems far too risky. Better to stay on the tried-and-true path, and not disappoint, than to veer off course and potentially fail. It's much more comfortable on cruise control.

However, your growth only stagnates when you allow yourself to wallow in the state of being stuck. As long as you are progressing, as we'll see in the next chapter, you are on the path to developing your voice.

Question: Where in your life and work are you on autopilot, or have you settled into a routine, overly familiar kind of action?

Awareness of these three hurdles, and the fossilization they cause, is crucial as we move on to strategies that we'll discuss next. It's important to understand the kinds of friction you will surely encounter as you strive to veer off the expected path. These hurdles will be constant nuisances on your journey, but you will overcome them as you cultivate your sense of identity, commit to a vision, and cultivate mastery.

CHECKPOINT

The challenge with each of the hurdles is that you might be completely unaware of how they've become infused into your mind-set, and thus affected your engagement. Having a set of questions to refer to can help you identify them and begin to countermand them.

EXCAVATION
Which of the hurdles discussed in this chapter (fear, narratives, inertia) might be holding you back from taking risks and developing your voice? How so?

OBSERVATION
Can you identify an instance in which you willfully held back, or didn't follow your intuition, because of one of these hurdles? What was it, and how did it affect your work?

Consider a specific upcoming scenario in which you are likely to encounter one of these hurdles. What is the situation, and how might that hurdle affect you?

REDIRECTION
As you consider the hurdle that most limits your ability to bring your best effort to your work, how will you confront it the next time it emerges? Think of a specific instance in which you are most likely to

experience that hurdle in the coming week, and formulate a strategy for how you will deal with it. This could mean grounding yourself in the true nature of the risk involved (rather than the perceived risk), replacing a limiting narrative with a more truthful one, or determining the first steps you'll take outside your comfort zone as a means to conquer mindless inertia.

Chapter 3

The Aspiration Gap

I was seeking comic originality, and fame fell on me as a
by-product. The course was more plodding than heroic:
I did not strive valiantly against doubters but took
incremental steps studded with a few intuitive leaps.

—Steve Martin, *Born Standing Up*

**Principle: As you develop your authentic voice, you will repeatedly experience
four phases of growth—Discovery, Emulation, Divergence, and Crisis.**

In an interview with Public Radio International in 2009, Ira Glass,
the host of the wildly popular radio program *This American Life*,
shared his thoughts on the struggles many people experience in the
field of creativity and making art. He said, "What nobody tells people
who are beginners—and I really wish someone had told this to me—
is that all of us who do creative work, we get into it because we have
good taste. But there is this gap. For the first couple of years you make

41

stuff, and it's just not that good. It's trying to be good, it has potential, but it's not."

Glass continued, "But your taste, the thing that got you into the game, is still killer. And your taste is why your work disappoints you. A lot of people never get past this phase. They quit. Most people I know who do interesting, creative work went through years of this. . . . It is only by going through a volume of work that you will close that gap, and your work will be as good as your ambitions." He closed with these words of encouragement: "It's going to take a while. It's normal to take a while. You've just got to fight your way through."

What Glass highlights so succinctly is a dynamic that I have dubbed the aspiration gap. This is the difference between the work that you want to create and the work that you're actually capable of creating at the moment, and it's the daily struggle of budding artists and writers, entrepreneurs, managers, and anyone else who desires to be unique and brilliant. When this gap exists, it's often due to high personal expectations founded in your observation of the work of other people you admire. When you are incapable of producing work that meets those high standards, it's tempting to give up far too soon. For this reason, many people either quit or move on to something more "reasonable" simply because they were frustrated by their temporary inability to achieve their vision. (As we saw in the previous chapter, this is often what happens in the bottom of the valley.)

I believe that closing the aspiration gap by developing your authentic voice is the primary job of any creative, and it's the primary focus of the remainder of this book. There are four phases that you will go through over and over as you strive to do so. These phases are experienced by anyone you can think of who embarks on a creative venture. They are also descriptive of how companies find their footing in the marketplace. I call them the phases of growth, and they are the path to uniqueness and mastery of your craft.

As Sarah Lewis wrote in her book *The Rise*, "Mastery, a word we don't use often, is not the equivalent of what we might consider its cognate—perfectionism—an inhuman aim motivated by a concern with how others view us. Mastery is also not the same as success—an event-based victory based on a peak point, a punctuated moment in time. Mastery is not merely a commitment to a goal, but to a curved-line, constant pursuit."

The process of developing your authentic voice is not linear, it is a curved line. There is an ebb and flow to growth, and you will often feel like you have to take a few steps backward in order to advance. This is because growth demands that you push yourself to your limits—and often beyond—in order to increase your capacity. A piano virtuoso will not continue to improve if she practices only the chords and scales that are easy for her, nor will a writer improve his craft if he stays squarely in his comfort zone. As the writer Joshua Foer put it, "When most musicians sit down to practice, they play the parts of pieces that they're good at. Of course they do: it's fun to succeed. But expert musicians tend to focus on the parts that are hard, the parts they haven't yet mastered." Most musicians get stuck in what Foer describes as the "OK Plateau," or a place of comfort where existing skills are good enough to suffice. However, because expert musicians are consistently stretching themselves to attempt new things, they discover new avenues of expression to explore, master, and implement into their own style. Over time, their platform for expression grows, and they are better prepared when the moment of opportunity arises. As they build their platform, they sharpen their instincts, and increase their ability to express themselves.

The same principle applies to nearly any kind of creative endeavor, but there's a strong catch involved: you must be willing to endure a period of incompetence, which may last months or even years, in order to see progress in closing the gap. No matter how successful you are, or how skillful you may be, stretching beyond your comfort zone will mean feeling "less than" for a time. How long this lasts depends on how complex the skill you're learning is, and how much context you already have for it. However, for many accomplished creators the sense of incompetence never fully goes away. As acclaimed author and cultural icon Kurt Vonnegut once quipped in an interview, "When I write, I feel like an armless, legless man with a crayon in his mouth." I don't get the sense that this was false modesty, but rather the genuine description of what a commitment to lifelong creative growth feels like.

Pushing to the edge of your ability is equivalent to stretching to the point of defeat, which means that failure will be a frequent companion on the road to eventual success. I think we accept this intellectually, but in practice it can be much more painful and demotivating. It's so much easier to coast on your existing skills and knowledge than to risk the appearance of incompetence that often comes with trying new things. However, while the sting of failure never fully goes away, over time you will come to see it as a natural and necessary part of the growth process.

THE "DEEP END" FALLACY

If your child wanted to learn to swim, would you tell him, "Just go jump into the deep end of the pool, and you'll figure it out"? Of course not! You know that without the basic building blocks to be able to swim, jumping in the deep end is deadly. However, we often hear stories of people who jumped into the metaphorical "deep end" in their line of work without any support, and came out on the other side as celebrated and successful. We love to tell those stories, but I think they can often be deceiving. It makes us believe that mastery and success is a by-product of blind risk taking rather than calculated, willful steps into the unknown.

Yes, developing your voice requires certain risk. You cannot grow without taking chances with your work. However, recognize that the most resonant, effective voices are developed over time through observation, practice, trial, error, and then eventual success. Most everyone starts in the shallow end by developing the basic building blocks, then they move on to more complicated and dangerous risks once they've mastered the basics.

Even masters of their craft frequently return to these basics, and go through the phases of growth over and over, in order to continue their journey toward greatness. In an interview with *Rolling Stone*, Rush drummer Neil Peart, widely considered to be one of the greatest rock-and-roll drummers ever, shared why he continued to take drum lessons even though he was at the peak of his career.

"What is a master but a master student? And if that's true, then there's a responsibility on you to keep getting better and to explore avenues of your profession. I've been put in this position, and I certainly don't underrate that. I get to be a professional drummer." This mind-set of continuous growth is what keeps the masters at the top of their game.

Just like everyone before you, there are four phases of growth you will experience as you develop your voice.

DISCOVERY PHASE

Imagine a man is at lunch one day, and over the restaurant speakers an Eric Clapton song begins playing in the background. He is transported back to his youth, and remembers that he once had a desire to learn how to play guitar. He considers how life might be different if he had taken up the guitar as a teenager, and begins imagining how much fun it would be to be able to sit down and play guitar as a form of relaxation and release. Then comes the epiphany: there's no reason he shouldn't begin now. There's no better time than the present to learn. With great excitement, he leaves work that day, walks to the local music store, and, after some haggling with the sales clerk, buys a decent starter guitar. The guitar even comes with a video tutorial that will help him learn the basics, like the main chords and scales needed to play a few songs. There is a noticeable pep in his step as he makes his way home, with guitar in tow, imagining how wonderful it will be to finally be able to replicate the music of his heroes. (He even begins thinking of possible band names for his soon-to-be megagroup.)

That evening after dinner, he pulls the guitar out of its case, and fires up the video. The instructor, a worn-out-looking raspy-voiced rock and roller, offers some quick tips about how to hold the guitar, how to use a pick, and how to tune the strings. After a half hour of noodling, he decides that this is good enough for one evening, and puts the guitar back in its case.

He repeats the same pattern over the coming few days, but soon, with a big work project on the horizon, the guitar emerges from the case less and less often. His fingertips are sore from the initial effort anyway, and he decides to put his guitar learning on hold for a month or so as he focuses on more urgent matters. The guitar is placed in the back of a closet, where it sits for a few months, largely untouched.

Our guitar-learner has just experienced an important phase of developing his voice as an artist. He has discovered a new skill he wishes to learn, and has even taken some early, awkward steps in the effort to grow. However, while his desire to learn is there, desire alone is not sufficient for growth. In order to develop his voice, he will have to instill a regimen that helps him learn the basic building blocks of his desired craft.

Questions that someone might ask during Discovery phase include:

What skill do I need to learn in order to achieve the next level of impact?

Where is my curiosity leading me next?

What platform do I need to develop so that I can achieve my vision?

What natural aptitude have I always wanted to improve upon, but haven't?

EMULATION PHASE

In this phase, you develop the basic building blocks of your craft by emulating others who have already achieved mastery. Through deliberate practice, you grow your platform for expression with grit and determination, even though the immediate payoff may not be proportionate to the amount of pain and effort you're putting in. You are, in a sense, "paying your dues." You are building the platform you will need later to develop and utilize your authentic voice.

As a child, one of the worst labels you could receive was to be called a copycat. The strange irony is that mimicking is the very mechanism by which each child learns to be unique. For example, early attempts to speak are efforts to mimic the sounds coming from parents and others, but once those basic communication skills become second nature, they are converted into building blocks for unique expression. You can't write a brilliant poem until you have mastered the basics of grammar, which begins with verbatim mimicking of the adults around you.

In his book *Mastery*, Robert Greene explores the apprenticeship-master model that dominated the Western economic system until only a few centuries ago. Under this model, a master tradesman would take on an apprentice (sometimes a family member, though often a young child given over by a family) to help with the daily labor of his business. It was a necessary mechanism for ensuring the future survival of the trades, and was also a hoped-for path to future prosperity for the family. In return for years of faithful service, the apprentice would receive training in a specific trade from the master. Through rigorous emulation, the apprentice would fumble through the basics of the craft until mastered, then move on to more intricate elements of the trade. At some point, most apprentices would achieve a sufficient level of skill to take on more complex work that previously only the master could do. Finally, the apprentice would be able to produce a "master piece," which was something of such quality that it was indistinguishable from the master's work. At this point, the apprentice would leave the apprenticeship and become master of a new shop, taking on apprentices of his own.

While the apprenticeship model is no longer the primary formal structure of our economic system, its principles still provide valuable guide rails for those who want to become unique masters of their craft. The problem is, few of us have the opportunity to work directly with a master and sit under their tutelage. However, now more than ever it is possible to position yourself at the feet of "virtual" masters, and develop your craft by emulating the work you admire. To do so you must immerse yourself in the work of your heroes, discern the qualities that make them exceptional, and adopt and emulate them until you too have achieved mastery.

This emulation of heroes is often pinpointed as a key element of how iconic creators developed their voice. Stephen King, the prolific novelist, has inspired near cultlike admiration from his legions of fans. In his book *On Writing*, in which he explores his own origins as an author and shares some advice for how to create noteworthy work, he wrote, "Imitation preceded creation; I would copy Combat Casey comics word for word in my Blue Horse tablet, sometimes adding my own descriptions where they seemed appropriate." His early emulation of the work he admired allowed him to refine his technique and discover what it felt like to create something great, even if it wasn't solely his own. Steve Earle, the brilliant songwriter, once quipped, "All we do as songwriters is rewrite the songs that have impressed us till we find our own voice. It's part of learning the craft." In her book on writing called *Steering the Craft*, novelist Ursula K. Le Guin also encourages budding authors to emulate the voices of their heroes, but offers this word of caution: "When imitating, it's necessary to remember the work, however successful, is practice, not an end in itself, but a mean towards the end of writing with skill and freedom in one's own voice." This lesson can be applied to any area in which you are emulating as a means of developing a platform of basic skills.

Back to our example of the man trying to learn guitar. After a few weeks, he decides that in spite of the inconvenience and the pain in his fingers, he really does want to learn how to play. His desire to improve overcomes his frustration. He knows that this means he must pull the guitar out of the closet, and commit to the hard work of learning the rudimentary building blocks, including notes, chords, and strumming. He sets some time each week to sit down with the guitar, watch the video, and copy what the instructor is teaching. He also sets some additional time to practice between these sessions, so that he can master these basic building blocks. At first, progress is slow and painful. His fingers continue to ache, and it seems that he is no better than when he began. However, after a month or so of continuous practice, he is able to form a few chords and even combine them into something resembling a song. This provides the motivation he needs to keep going. Small wins provide the encouragement to continue, and show that basic competence is within his reach. After six months of consistent effort, he's become much more proficient, and has mastered the basic building blocks covered in the video.

This is a critical stage, because what he does next can either make or break his ambitions. How does he continue growing? By closely listening to and emulating other people who are still further along the path. Perhaps he studies the music of one of his favorite bands, and slowly begins picking out chords on the guitar until he can approximate what he is hearing. He may purchase a book that teaches more advanced chords and strumming patterns. He will continue to develop his platform by emulating those who are more advanced. Emulation phase will continue until he is comfortable with many of the basics and becomes so adept that they can be performed almost unconsciously. Though he's not yet a master, his deliberate practice gives him the building blocks he'll eventually need to fire off Clapton-like guitar solos for his friends. In fact, not only is playing guitar no longer painful and awkward, it has actually become second nature.

However, emulation can also be a sticking point. Once you develop basic competence, it's easy to coast. After all, basic competence is often enough to get you much of what you want in terms of a steady job, stable income, and general comfort. This love of comfort can be dangerous.

A lot of the work that you create during Emulation phase is not for public consumption. Rather, it's work that you are doing to try on new styles, develop your skills, and grow your ability to use the basic building blocks of your craft. You are acting as an "apprentice" of the work that you admire. This might mean closely mimicking the voice or tone of another person, imitating a leader you admire, or building the deliberate practice of your craft into your daily regimen so that you are growing your platform of expression.

Questions you might ask during Emulation phase include:

Who are the masters of the skill I'm learning or platform I'm building?

What works should I immerse myself in so that I can get a better sense of my own taste and vision for my work?

What are the building blocks I should emulate, and how can I practice them deliberately and often?

DIVERGENCE PHASE

Once you have achieved a level of competence and comfort with the building blocks of your craft, you face a difficult challenge. It's at this point that you must decide whether you will continue to "stay in your lane" or take the risks necessary to push into new territory. It's time to begin taking small, calculated, public risks and using your acquired skills as the launchpad for self-expression. Until now, in Emulation phase, you were mostly mimicking the work of others in order to find your footing. Now, however, it's time to use the muscles you've developed to put your own spin on things. You will never develop your voice if you choose to stay in familiar places doing familiar things. You must commit to sailing perpendicular to the shoreline if you want to truly shine.

Divergence is about using the basic platform you've built during emulation to push even further outside your comfort zone, often with little guaranteed return. Because of the lack of certainty, many people never move into this phase of growth. It's much easier to stay squarely in familiar territory, where you know that your efforts will achieve some measure of return, even if it's a small one.

How do you know when it's time to diverge?

You sense a general level of dissatisfaction with your work.

You feel that you could be doing more, but you've reached the limit of your ability to influence given your existing arena of influence. To get to where you ultimately want to be, you know you have to change how you are approaching your work, even if you don't yet know what that means.

This is not necessarily—as some interpret it—a dissatisfaction with the tasks that comprise your work. It's easy to confuse mode of work with output, and thus some people spend their lives running away from work that is uncomfortable or foreign, when the most valuable thing for them to do would be to dive headlong into it. If you want to grow, you must move toward opportunities, not just away from pain points.

You have a growing sense of resentment for your heroes and mentors. An odd thing happens when you become highly skilled at the basics of your craft. Often, the very influences that you cherished as you were learning your craft begin to lose their shine. Whenever a writer turns a phrase that smacks of one of her heroes, she feels resentful. When a leader parrots a phrase that was once used by a mentor, it feels flat. Suddenly the very tools that enabled you to get to a place of fluency are no longer sufficient to get you where you want to be. You may start to pick apart your heroes or use them as a point of differentiation for your own work. You can no longer stay in emulation mode if you want to grow.

Containers start to feel suffocating. Generally speaking, as you go about your work, you are either creating new containers or filling existing ones. For many people, the early years are spent building containers for their work, and then they labor for years to fill them. (Think of a writer who creates a blog as a container for his thoughts, or a manager who creates a new organization for an initiative, then spends several years working inside that container.) However, over time the containers themselves can begin to stale or feel stifling. When you are no longer excited about the container you are filling, it is possibly a sign that it's time to move on and build a new one. If you choose to stay and continue on your current course, you are likely to grow stagnant.

You see an opportunity you can't refuse. The final indication that it's time to begin taking public risks with your work is when an opportunity presents itself that, while clearly beyond your current capability, you simply cannot refuse. This opportunity demands that you step outside your comfort zone, and there is a very real potential for failure, but you know that if you refuse it you are likely to regret it down the line. The potential upside is worth the leap.

It is never easy to make these strategic leaps, regardless of how many times you've done it before. As noted researcher and author Mihaly Csikszentmihalyi wrote in his seminal work *Creativity*, "Each of us is born with two contradictory sets of instructions: a conservative tendency, made up of instincts for self-preservation, self-aggrandizement, and saving energy, and an expansive tendency made up of instincts for exploring, for enjoying novelty and risk—the curiosity that leads to creativity belongs to this set. We need both of these programs. But whereas the first tendency requires little encouragement or support from outside to motivate behavior, the second can wilt if it is not cultivated." The key to Divergence phase is to take small risks on a regular basis so that—while never easy—you begin to grow more comfortable with the potential of failure.

Let's return once again to our example of the man learning guitar. At some point, he will have mastered enough of the basic building blocks to afford him the ability to begin experimenting and developing his own style. During his practice times, he begins taking small risks when playing in order to stretch himself. He starts playing for his friends, and maybe joins a band. In addition, he begins listening to and copying different musical styles, then incorporating them into his play. He even adds a touch of his own style, including a mix of his now extensive musical influences, when playing the songs he previously emulated verbatim. In short, he is discovering and applying his own voice. He is slowly closing the aspiration gap.

Each phase requires that you commit to small daily activities that continue to push you up the growth curve toward finding your authentic voice. To put it another way, you need to place a series of what author Peter Sims terms "little bets," or small but strategic risks, to assess the viability of various ideas. Sims referenced comedian Chris Rock, who regularly tests his new material in smaller comedy clubs in front of very critical audiences before taking his show on the road and performing to thousands of people at a time. This allows Rock to learn on the fly and tweak his timing and delivery in a relatively low-risk environment many times instead of taking one big risk in front of a large crowd in an unfamiliar city.

Don't buy into the myth that developing your voice requires big, unconventional leaps into the unknown, and a devil-may-care attitude about the consequences. If you believe that you have been given something unique to contribute to the world, then you have the accompanying responsibility to help it gain as much of the right audience as you can.

The more of these little bets you place along the way, the more you grow in your understanding of how to exercise your voice, and the better you will be positioned to take advantage of an opportunity when it comes along. Also, as you become a student of your own ability to influence others, you will become much more proficient at recognizing new opportunities as well.

Questions you might ask during Divergence phase include:

> What strategic risk will I take with my work today, and how will I know I succeeded?

Where do I feel dissatisfied with my current level of performance, and what can I do differently to push myself out of my comfort zone?

Where are the opportunities that I've been ignoring, but know I need to pursue?

CRISIS PHASE

Inevitably, your work will grow stale. It happens to everyone. Over time, what you're producing seems inexplicably less satisfying. In short, you are in a rut, and you may even feel a bit burned out. Often, this is because you lack the sense of challenge that you experienced during times of extreme growth. You've hit the point where your existing skills offer you a diminishing return, and you may even have grown bored with your work. After all the diverging, risk taking, and effort to develop your voice, you've suddenly hit an impasse. You are stuck and there doesn't seem to be a path forward. However, just plowing through the block isn't necessarily the answer. Instead, it often helps to step back, consider your situation, and think about the places where you might be stuck. This will give you an understanding of new skills to develop or new questions to ask that will open up unexplored avenues of growth. Digging faster will not get you out of the hole.

The true challenge of Crisis phase is this: others might not notice it. Your friends and peers might tell you that your work is great, and it may still be on par with the best in your field. However, deep down you know that you are no longer growing and that you've settled into a pattern of safety and comfort.

At this point, you have two choices: you can either remain stagnant, using the same methods and skills to tackle the work that's in front of you and continuing on your present course, or you can intentionally return to Discovery phase and challenge yourself to develop a new skill or means of expression. If you do the former, you are likely to begin a slow decline into mediocrity and misery. If you do the latter, you will be uncomfortable for a while, but you will continue growing.

I call this Crisis phase because it marks a critical line in the development of voice. It can be difficult to make a clean break from your old habits, methods, and ideas and move on to something that feels foreign and uncomfortable, but that's precisely what you have to do if you want to push through Crisis phase and continue developing. If you wallow in Crisis phase without taking action, you are likely to stagnate and eventually become less effective and motivated. If you are not growing, you will not stay at the same level of impact, and you will eventually decline.

To close the loop on our guitar-playing friend, once he reaches Crisis phase he must again push himself out of his comfort zone and stretch himself to the point of incompetence. Perhaps he must learn a different stringed instrument that will complement his guitar-playing ability. Maybe he needs to learn how to play a different kind of guitar in order to get a more unique tone. The key is that he must not allow himself to remain in a rut, but must commit to continuing his journey of growth.

Questions you might ask during Crisis phase include:

Where am I stuck, and what decisions got me there?

What new idea or avenue excites me, but I am ignoring for practical reasons?

What is the next frontier of growth for me, in order to continue pursuing mastery of my craft?

It's tempting to believe that the people we most admire for their voice emerged from the womb with a special ability for expression. We believe that they have somehow been kissed by the gods or that they have an extra-special ability to hear the call of the Muses, and thus have a supernatural leaning toward brilliance. It doesn't help that our mythology surrounding these great contributors often includes the infamous aha moment, when they had the sudden realization that changed everything in their work. We oversimplify our cultural myths about how brilliant work emerges to the point that the myths themselves become a paralyzing force. As author Jon Acuff puts it, "Don't compare your beginning to someone else's middle."

Of course, raw talent accounts for a varying portion of success and can't be discounted, but I think that we sometimes overemphasize talent at the expense of more important factors, like self-awareness and grit. I'll place my bet on a committed person who refuses to settle over a prodigy who is phoning it in. Developing your voice requires (a) a willingness to embrace curious exploration of your life and work, and (b) the grit to persistently do hard things that have no immediate payoff, trusting that the benefits will come over time.

As we move into the next section of the book, and begin to discuss how Identity, Vision, and Mastery drive the development of your authentic voice, keep these four phases of growth in mind. Consider how you might apply the practices you learn within the context of where you are on the growth curve. Honor the phases of growth, and commit to daily activities that will keep you moving in the right direction, and you will—eventually—reap the rewards as you close the aspiration gap.

CHECKPOINT

These phases are not necessarily discreet stages of growth with clear lines separating them. Rather, they are descriptors of the general phases of struggle you will face as you develop your voice. That said, understanding where you might be in your arc of growth can help you identify the kinds of activities that will keep you moving forward in the discovery of your authentic voice, and help you avoid becoming stagnant or stuck. The following questions and actions are designed to help you assess next steps.

EXCAVATION

Is there any area in your life where you feel that you've succumbed to the "OK Plateau," as described by Joshua Foer? Why do you think you've settled in that area?

As you consider the four phases (Discovery, Emulation, Divergence, Crisis) can you identify some areas of your work and craft where you are in each of them?

OBSERVATION

In those areas you've identified, what is the next action for you in order to continue growing? (If you are in Discovery phase, what specific, repeatable practices can you build through emulation? If you are in Emulation phase, think of how you can begin taking small, strategic risks to follow your intuition. If you are in Divergence phase, consider the places where you are most likely to grow stagnant so that you can build a bulwark against it. If you are in Crisis phase, consider which new skill you might want to develop so that you can continue on your arc of growth.)

As you consider where your work is taking you, what new skills do you need to develop over the coming months or few years in order to allow you to take advantage of opportunities? List a few new skills that you know you will need to focus on in order to continue developing your voice.

REDIRECTION

Build time into your weekly rhythm for acting on the items you listed above. Schedule intentional playtime, time to develop new skills, and time to break away and listen to your intuition and follow your curiosity. How can you establish a regular routine that enables you to devote time to helping you move up the growth curve?

PART 2

The Voice Engine

Developing your authentic voice is not just about personal gratification, it's about achieving impact. In order to do that, your work must resonate with others. You must be mindful of not only what you want to communicate but also how it will be received by your audience.

In this section, you'll learn about how the three parts of the Voice Engine drive the development of your authentic voice, and how they allow your work to resonate with the people you serve.

When your voice resonates, the impact you achieve speaks louder than the words you use.

Chapter 4

Identity: Who Are You?

I have often thought the best way to define a man's character would be to seek out the particular mental or moral attitude in which, when it comes upon him, he felt himself most deeply and intensely active and alive. At such moments there is a voice inside which speaks and says: "This is the real me!"

—William James

Principle: For your voice to resonate, it must be rooted in authenticity and uniqueness.

"I think my through-line has always been publishing," Jocelyn Glei told me, "but that only became clear looking backward." Glei, who is the former director of the Webby Award—winning creative think tank and publisher 99U, said that the early signs of her love of publishing began showing up in high school. "I used to have my own zine that I would be embarrassed to show anyone now, but I created a matching shirt and logo, and really was into it." In college, Glei studied both literature and film while interning at MIT Press and at a central services office where she helped various departments get their work published. It was here that Glei first learned about the importance of the design aspects of publishing. "I didn't realize at the time that would be so important, but it turns out it really mattered later." Through a friend of a friend, she ended up in a role at a small Web design firm operating in a "jane-of-all-trades" role, preparing databases, photos, and other items for publication on the Web. Unfortunately, her company was caught up in the "dot bomb" crash, and when she lost her job, she decided to move to New York to expand her career options.

As her first step in a new city, Glei volunteered at *Flavorpill*, an online publication that focuses on cultural events listings, where she eventually came to manage an editorial team of twenty people. "It was here that all of my previous experiences, from publishing to Web site building to design, started to come together." Glei was at *Flavorpill* for five years before she decided to leave and make a go at freelance work. In one of her first projects, while helping a friend launch a Web site, she met Scott Belsky, an entrepreneur who had just landed a book deal and needed some help with research and editing. Scott is cofounder of Behance, an online portfolio site for creative pros, and had just started a new brand called 99U. "After [Scott's] book launched, we realized we really liked working together. The very first 99U Conference had already happened, and together we essentially decided to turn it into an online brand." Glei joined Behance to lead the launch of the 99U Web site, which over subsequent years has yielded more conferences, books, international meetups, and a raving worldwide audience of millions. When I asked her how she was able to find her way into a role that is so perfectly suited to her unique skills and passions, she said, "I think there is a sort of relentless desire in me to be asking 'what's next?' and to keep pushing forward. If you stop asking that question, you stall. However, if you're always thinking about what's next, then it allows you to move toward areas where you can find work that's uniquely suited to your skill set. It's about following your through-line."

What Glei refers to as her "through-line" is a central theme, or grounding understanding of who she is and what she offers the world. It isn't something she's fabricated, but something that she uncovered over time as she's experimented, made things, succeeded and failed, and paid close attention along the way. A through-line is discernible looking backward, but not always looking forward, which is why you often have to pay attention to patterns that reveal themselves in your past experiences in order to identify it.

Your through-line is an important marker of identity. It's a grounding element that helps you refine your vision, and it provides a sense of purpose and drive for your work. A compelling, authentic voice is rooted in a strong sense of identity.

Have you ever stopped to consider when you have been most engaged and effective? When have others responded most profoundly or resonated most deeply with you? Or, perhaps most telling of all, when have you felt the most alive when engaged in the process of creating something of value? Connecting these dots can help you discern the through-line for your work. It's often not what it may appear to be on the surface or to others.

In his book *The Element*, in which he explores the lives and careers of people who have contributed uniquely to the world, Ken Robinson describes the state of operating according to a through-line as "the Element." It's the place, Robinson argues, where your natural talent meets your personal passion. He writes, "Being good at something and having passion for it are essential to finding the Element. But they are not enough. Getting there depends fundamentally on our view of ourselves and of the events in our lives." What Robinson is getting at is that identifying your unique offering and aligning it with your passion is not sufficient in and of itself to create impact. Compelling work and a clear, true voice have deep roots. There are two key aspects of identity that, when infused into your work, drive resonance with your audience: authentic investment and uniqueness.

AUTHENTICITY: PUTTING "SKIN IN THE GAME"

Edward Bernays is known to many as the father of public relations, but he can equally be considered the originator of modern propaganda. Beginning in the early 1920s and continuing for decades thereafter, he mastered the art of manipulation through references to authority, strategic press releases, and Pavlovian techniques designed to manipulate the masses into action favorable to his clients. Not only was he a proponent of this kind of mass manipulation, but he considered it necessary for the proper operation of a democratic society. In the opening lines of his seminal work, *Propaganda*, he wrote, "The conscious and intelligent manipulation of the organized habits and opinions of the masses is an important element in democratic society. Those who manipulate this unseen mechanism of society constitute an invisible government which is the true ruling power of our country."

He continued, "We are governed, our minds are molded, our tastes formed, our ideas suggested, largely by men we have never heard of. This is a logical result of the way in which our democratic society is organized. Vast numbers of human beings must cooperate in this manner if they are to live together as a smoothly functioning society." Bernays believed an ideal society is shaped by an invisible ruling elite, of which he was a part. However, over the past several decades, the very society that Bernays strove to manipulate has grown skeptical of agendas, marketing messages, and false promises. Today, most people default to "looking for the angle" when examining an idea, which means that it is harder than ever to gain trust and credibility. We have been warped by decades of positioning and inauthentic pitches. While it's nearly impossible to win over everybody, the key to overcoming the skeptics and cynics is to operate from a place of authenticity. What people really want to know when they interact with your work is "Do they really believe what they are saying? Are they really invested?"

What does this have to do with developing your voice? Everything, if you want your work to resonate with your audience. You have to know what you believe, what you stand for, and what you're willing to invest yourself in (fully) if you want your work to stand against the onslaught of skepticism and critique. A unique, compelling voice isn't about manipulation, it's about influence, which ultimately begins with a firm understanding of yourself and what matters to you.

To identify your through-line, and then to cultivate authentic investment, it helps to first identify the resonant themes within your work, then distill those themes into a personal operating manual, or working manifesto, that is designed to help you stay on course while potentially attracting others to your mission as well.

THE 50 NOTABLES

In Greek mythology, the nine Muses were the beings who personified the creative arts. Each Muse worked within her specific domain, and inspired writing, poetry, dance, and music. Artists throughout history have turned to the Muses for a breakthrough, pleading with them to bring fresh ideas when they are stuck.

Here's what I find interesting about this myth: the Muses were the offspring of Zeus, the king of the gods and power, and Mnemosyne, who was memory personified. Thus, with amazing insight into the actual inner workings of the human mind, the Greeks believed that creativity resulted from applying energy to memory, or taking existing bits of past experience and intentionally applying them to new problems in order to discover fresh ideas. Creativity is fundamentally about combining existing stimuli in your environment—experiences, pieces of knowledge, other problems you've solved, similar situations you've been in, things you've read about—and playing around with them until you find a combination that helps you solve the problem you're focused on. As Apple cofounder Steve Jobs once famously quipped, "Creativity is just connecting things." This definition of creativity implies that the better the stimuli in your mind, and the more adept you become at playing with them, the more effectively you will be able to generate ideas. It is also true that playing with the stimuli in your environment, and recognizing how you respond to them, is a great way to identify a through-line for your work, and cultivate a sense of identity.

Play is an important part of growth. In childhood, it's the fundamental mechanism for learning about the nature of the world, for testing limits, and for building strength. As we grow older, we are conditioned (typically through the education system and early experiences in the workforce) to spend less time experimenting and more time efficiently seeking the right answer. This means that many potentially valuable roads are left unexplored, and we move on so quickly that we never have time to reflect on our experiences and what they mean to who we are and where we are going. However, when we take the time to stop and examine those experiences, we often find common and resonant themes present within those times when we are most effective and alive.

How often do you take time to step back and look at the patterns in your life? In the fray of day-to-day activity, it's easy to forget to do this. There are limitless demands for your attention, with the unwelcome result being a pervasive numbness to your surroundings. Though you may have brief moments of insight or inspiration, they are quickly swallowed by the next task. Observations that you believe to be profound one moment soon fold into the background noise and are forgotten.

However, these moments of insight often point to a deeper pattern of recognition that could lead you to a breakthrough, or help you to better understand your authentic voice. It's important to take note of not only what you are doing but how you are responding emotionally, mentally, and physically to the work. Your through-line often becomes clear only as you connect seemingly unrelated dots. To make those connections, you must pay attention to experiences in your life and work and consider how they might be relevant to your overall objectives. This helps you identify sources of inspiration, new skills to learn, and patterns for exploration as you develop your voice.

One practice that I often prescribe is called 50 Notables. It uses five categories of questions to help you identify areas where you personally come alive in your work, or where your work is especially resonant with others. I'd encourage you to take a few minutes with a sheet of paper to do this exercise now. For each question below, jot down the first ten answers that come to mind.

1. When are you at your best? When do others seem to connect most deeply to your ideas? What is the context, whom does the idea tend to inspire, and why do you think that's the case? Try to keep listing until you come up with ten specific instances.

2. When are you moved emotionally? List the last ten times you can recall getting emotional about something you experienced, whether at work, at home, or with friends. Use a few words to describe the circumstances and why you were moved.

3. What stirs your anger? I don't mean road rage, I'm talking about compassionate anger. *Compassion* means to "suffer with," or that you're angry on behalf of someone else who has been wronged, or a situation in which you felt for someone else. List ten times when you have been moved with compassionate anger.

4. What gives you great hope? When have you taken a position that others have deemed crazy, but you held firm in spite of their skepticism? Where do you hold a strong vision and great hope for your life and work, even though it may seem irrational to others? List ten of them, if there are that many.

5. What kinds of problems are you naturally drawn to solving? When you look at your life and your work, what are the qualities of the problems you tend to gravitate toward? What do you find yourself doing even though you don't have to? What kinds of problems do you naturally obsess over? List ten instances, if possible, when you became obsessed with solving a problem.

Now that you have a list of (approximately) fifty notables, begin looking for themes. Can you see any patterns emerging within your best moments, your emotional moments, your anger, your hope, and your obsessions?

These five categories are a great calibration tool to help you figure out how to direct your work, where to look for opportunities to explore, and which kinds of skills you should be developing. As an ongoing exercise, I'd challenge you to continue to pay attention to notables in your environment. Remember that your best work, and your most resonant, authentic voice, will result from a deep self-knowledge. It's possible that these notable, voice-shaping experiences show up far more often than you would expect. Keep a running log of things you see, experience, or otherwise come across that move or challenge you. For example, things that:

Spark a new insight

Make you angry

Excite you

Surprise you

Concern you

Make you aspire to something

Make you afraid

You can also forage through your memories for notable events, moments of victory or defeat, and other sorts of highs and lows. Here are a few examples that might prompt items for your list:

Key memories or life moments. Sometimes something happens during your day that reminds you of a similar experience from long ago. It's easy to brush off these moments of nostalgia (or terror), but it can be helpful to pay attention to why you made the connection. Perhaps there is a valuable insight or pattern that might prove helpful in your work. Record it, and consider why it came to mind. Is there a pattern, or something potentially valuable to learn from it? Is there a theme to tap into?

Ideas or quotes from articles or books. When you're reading, it's possible that you'll come across something that uniquely resonates for one reason or another. You may even stop for a moment to admire and consider the idea. Instead of letting it slip away, take time to record it, and consider how it applies to your life and work.

Conversations. This is where a lot of my notables occur. I'm talking with someone—a client, a peer, a friend—and they say something that stuns me in its clarity. Or, because I tend to process my thoughts verbally, I might say something off the cuff in a conversation that I didn't realize I thought or felt. I try to capture these as soon as the conversation ends, because if I don't they will fade from my memory.

Great stories. One of the benefits of the always interconnected world is that you probably encounter a lot of great stories daily. Often these stories are inspiring, cautionary, or otherwise resonant, but you may experience them and then immediately move on to the next thing without considering how they could affect your work. Instead, capture your thoughts about them.

Meeting dynamics. Meetings are a fertile field for observations and potential ideas. Pay attention to the interpersonal dynamics in the room, to who takes up the lion's share of the attention, and to subtle prompts and thoughts you have as you interact with others. Also, pay attention to the moments when you are inspired to speak up, but don't, or speak when you probably shouldn't have. Why is that the case?

People watching. Often the best moments of clarity happen while in line at a coffee shop or while sitting in an airport. Take note of things that seem out of the ordinary or that spark an unusual thought or emotion and write them down. Remember that your authentic voice is sourced in your response to your environment, and your sense of identity is the narrative you tell yourself about your place in the world.

THE PROCESS OF CAPTURING NOTABLES

I used to capture notables throughout the day in my notebook with a star symbol beside each item, indicating that they were important thoughts or ideas. The problem was that these notables were scattered throughout my notebooks, which made identifying patterns extremely difficult. Over time, I began keeping them in a list with a little more structure so that I could refer to them often and note what might be happening beneath the surface of my consciousness.

Author Steven Johnson has written about his practice of keeping what he calls a spark file, which is a document containing observations, hunches, incomplete thoughts, and half-baked ideas. He makes it a habit to regularly reread this file to see if any of his previous ideas or observations are relevant to what he's currently working on. In doing this, he is leveraging the power of notables in his environment to bolster his work and refine his voice. You can do the same thing in a notebook, or using any number of pieces of software designed for note taking. However, the key is to make it a habit to record ideas and insights as they occur, and to regularly review them for patterns that spark inspiration.

You can keep your running list of notables anywhere that works best for you, but I've found that keeping them in the notebook I always carry with me ensures that I don't have to jump through too many hoops in order to write something down. The less friction is involved, the more likely you'll actually do it.

As a starting point, create four columns on the page. At the head of each column, write "Date," "What is it?" "Why notable?" and "Where." Over time, you can use shorthand, or get rid of the tags altogether, but at the beginning having the titles will help you stick with the structure.

Under "What is it?" write the experience or observation that resonated with you.

Under "Why notable?" record which of the five categories it fell under. Did it move you emotionally? Was it a problem that sparked your curiosity?

Under "Where" simply write where it happened. (Geographical clues will help you to remember it later, or to relive the experience.)

Take a bit of time each week to glance at your running list and see if you can identify any patterns. What sorts of things seem to catch your attention more than others? For example, there was a period of time a few years ago when I was noticing what made certain people I was interacting with able to speak with clarity and mobilize others toward an objective, and those patterns eventually distilled into the outline that became this book. Maybe you'll notice that your anger is being stirred in a particular area, or that you've been more emotional lately about a certain project. Pay attention to these things. What could they be pointing to, and what do they mean for how you direct your work?

As you review your list of notable things, ask yourself a few questions to help you identify themes:

What keeps coming up over and over? Do you find that you are documenting similar things again and again? Are there any similarities between them?

What applies to your present work? Is there anything on your list of notables that applies to the work in front of you? You'll find over time that some of your most effective ideas will result from applying old thoughts to new opportunities.

What emotions are you experiencing the most? Why do you think this is the case?

This is not intended to be deep psychoanalysis, to diagnose neuroses, or to identify a forgotten childhood trauma. It's just a simple practice to help you identify notable patterns so that you can apply that knowledge in shaping your voice, and thus the themes and arc of your work.

Once you've begun to identify some resonant themes, it can also help to distill them into a working manifesto.

A LIVING CREED

Don and I met over coffee. He'd been informed that his employment at his current company would be ending in the coming months, but his next steps were uncertain. He had a lot of experience in his field and a ton of talent, and frankly, any company would be lucky to have him. However, he was hesitant to just jump back into the same kind of job he had before, where he felt like his ability to influence others was more limited than he desired. I could see that he had a strong sense of where he wanted to take his life and work next, but he was having a lot of difficulty putting it into words. His language was vague, and the more he talked, the more it seemed like he was making himself more unsure of which direction to go.

"Have you ever tried writing your manifesto?" I asked.

"What's that mean?"

"It's a short document that captures the essence of who you are, what you stand for, and where you're headed," I explained. "It's kind of like a living creed that helps you and those you interact with know what you're about."

Don said he was willing to give it a shot. Over the coming few weeks he spent about fifteen minutes each day toiling away at his manifesto, and then after about a month he sent me his draft. "It's too vague," I told him. "I don't know if I believe you. Write it so that it scares you a little."

This is advice I've given many others over time. If you are not a little intimidated by your own manifesto, then it's unlikely that others will be moved by it either.

Don went back to writing, and when he returned to me with his finished draft I could see that something had changed. The cloudiness of his previous draft had evaporated. His passive language was active. More than that, Don seemed to have a newfound sense of hope about his career shift. Now that his manifesto was in place, he had a grounding set of principles to guide him on the next phase of his journey.

I've seen this happen many times with teams and individuals. I can tell they have something profound brewing inside, but when I try to get it out of them their words are muddy because their enthusiasm overshadows their clarity. Perhaps it's clear in their own minds, but they haven't given sufficient thought to the implications of their thoughts and beliefs and how others might receive them. All they needed was a structure to help them channel their passion into something more action oriented and easily shared. They needed a manifesto.

THE QUALITIES OF A GOOD MANIFESTO

Like most people with whom I share this concept, when you hear the word *manifesto*, your mind probably conjures up images of political phenomena and large-scale cultural movements. In fact, these are great examples of how a manifesto can be used to rally people around a cause and inspire action toward a desired end. Typically each of the above examples has a codified set of beliefs that participants adhere to. The manifesto is the aspirational glue that often holds these movements together. It is also the right tool to keep your actions aligned around the desired change you want to see through your work.

A manifesto is not the same as a mission statement, which sometimes tends to be general, almost to the point of irrelevance. It tries to encapsulate every possible permutation and circumstance, because its objective is to provide a broad-strokes path forward for an organization. A manifesto, on the other hand, captures why you are invested in your work, and acts as a continued compass for decisive action. It stands as a testament to the areas in which you are personally invested.

In his autobiography, famed architect Frank Lloyd Wright shared the manifesto he offered to his apprentices:

1. An honest ego in a healthy body
2. An eye to see nature
3. A heart to feel nature
4. Courage to follow nature
5. The sense of proportion (humor)
6. Appreciation of work as idea and idea as work
7. Fertility of imagination
8. Capacity for faith and rebellion

9. Disregard for commonplace (inorganic) elegance
10. Instinctive cooperation

While this list might at first seem vague to the uninitiated, it's easy to imagine the kinds of conversations it would inspire among the apprentices when kept at the forefront of daily activity. It provides guideposts for how to approach decisions, and how to seek inspiration when you are stuck. With regard to your sense of identity, your manifesto provides guide rails for you as you develop your voice. (For more examples of great manifestos, visit toddhenry.com/louder thanwords.)

WRITING YOUR MANIFESTO

What change do you want to see in the world through your work? What value do you want to create? How will you know that you were successful? These are the kinds of questions that your manifesto will be designed to address. It will not be a static statement of intent; it is likely to evolve and change over time as you learn more about yourself and the kind of impact you want to have. However, it provides you with two things: a constant, grounding document you can return to for inspiration and help in focusing, and an easy way to introduce others to what you care about. Your manifesto is like an antirésumé. It's reflective of where you're headed, not where you've been.

What is the message that's burning so intensely in you that you corner others and force them to listen to you ramble on about it at a dinner party? What is so important to you that when inspiration strikes you in the middle of the night, you find yourself getting out of bed and taking action because you can't sleep until you do? These are the sorts of things that will find expression in your manifesto, but you will have to wrestle high concepts into something more concrete and communicable.

While manifestos take many forms, there are a few principles that will help you in crafting one. In essence, there are three elements reflected in your manifesto statements: the who, the what, and the why.

Who: This is the audience for your work. Whom are you trying to reach? What problems are they facing that you're going to help them with? Regardless of the kind of work you do, its impact will ultimately be measured in terms of how it moves or serves others. As such, even if they are not overtly mentioned in the language of your manifesto, your desired audience should be implicit.

Often, I find that when people or teams are stuck when trying to generate ideas or strategy, it's because they haven't clearly defined precisely who it is they are serving through their work. As a result, they spin their wheels trying desperately to will progress, but traction won't come. This happens because they've lost sight of the people they are ultimately serving through their efforts. Once they refocus on who, it makes the problems they are solving much more tangible.

What: This is the actionable part of your manifesto. What do you do that adds value to the world, and serves your core audience? What specific values do you want to inject into the cultural conversation through your work? How do you provide value to the people you serve? What will be the tangible evidence of your action through your work?

Why: The most powerful manifestos have a "so that..." component, even if it isn't explicitly called out in the words. They are powered by something other than self-service, and reflect a deep belief about the way the world should be. Why do you want the people you serve to act? What tangible difference will exist in the world if they do? In fact, why should they listen to you at all? Your passion for your work must be communicated in your manifesto.

As I mentioned, these elements may not show up in your manifesto in tangible form. The worst thing would be for your manifesto to feel like a Frankenstein's monster of buzzwords, or like a forced corporate mission statement that looks impressive carved into a marble wall but has absolutely no bearing in reality. It should be something you live and breathe, and something that is so natural to you that others you know would read it and say "Yes . . . that's definitely you."

Developing authentic investment in your work is ultimately about getting in touch with your core drivers and the deepest sense of why you do what you do. Once you are able to tap into this deep well, you will be able to apply that new understanding to your work, and make it resonate more deeply with your audience. You will grow increasingly comfortable with who you are and the value you have to offer. You will no longer need to pretend to be something you're not, because you will recognize that the greatest thing of value you have to offer is your true self.

MAKE BOLD, UNIQUE DECISIONS

Amos Heller spent most of his twenties and early thirties playing bass guitar with a variety of bands in his hometown. Because of his skill and versatility, he quickly became known as a go-to player for live and session work. Though he was finding great success on the local level as a bass player, he still needed to supplement his music making with a job as a barista at a local coffee shop. After a few years of picking up gigs in the evening and serving coffee during the day, Amos decided the market simply wasn't big enough to support his desire to play music full-time. "Even though I wasn't the top dog in the city, I could see the top dog from where I was, and I realized that it wasn't really going to be enough even if I got there." He knew that if he wanted to expand his horizons, he would be well served to move to a city with a more thriving music scene, so with some encouragement from a friend, Amos set his sights on Nashville.

Quickly after moving, Amos managed to get a job at a coffee shop, and began searching for work as a bass player. "I realized that I had everything to learn, and everything to prove. Everyone here is hot stuff where they came from, but they traded that all in to come here, because no one knows who you are. You are starting from scratch." In the evening, he would visit clubs featuring live music and try to ingratiate himself to other musicians in the attempt to "crack the code" of breaking into the music business. He would trap musicians at the bar by buying them a drink, then pepper them with questions about how they got their gig, what advice they had for a newbie, etc. On one such occasion, a new acquaintance asked Amos what he was looking to do.

"I'll do anything!" Amos replied.

With a puzzled look on his face, his new friend informed Amos that this was not a useful response. Simply opening himself to "anything" would make it challenging to recommend him when opportunities emerged. Instead, he told Amos to be much more specific in what he was hoping to find. Amos thought for a moment, and said, "I want to be one of those guys on a bus I see traveling down the highway at two A.M. on their way to the next show." Therefore, they agreed that Amos was seeking an "artist gig," a term for employment as a supporting band member for a touring act. "That gave me a goal to help me clarify what I wanted to accomplish in my career," Amos told me. "To that point, I felt like I was spending a lot of energy in a lot of directions, but was making little headway."

About a year after he moved to Nashville, Amos got his first real artist gig. He received a call from a friend who said an opportunity opened up in a cover band that was touring the Southwest, playing mostly at Native American casinos. Amos said this was a kind of "farm league" for touring players, and was not in any way glamorous, but he was grateful for the chance to learn the ropes of being on the road and to simply be playing music for a living. "Looking back, I'm really glad that my chance to tour as a musician wasn't playing for fifteen thousand people in an arena, but instead playing for fifteen people who may or may not be listening to you. I really found my sea legs and refined my understanding of who I was as a player."

When that gig ended, he got a short one playing in a bar in Nashville, which led to a slightly more prestigious artist gig. As often happens in the music industry, which is largely network driven, that short-lived job led to another, and another, and soon Amos was gaining a reputation around town as a dependable sideman. When one of his friends shared that he would be leaving his role as touring bass player for country music star Taylor Swift in 2007, Amos asked that his name be tossed into the hat as a possible replacement. Fortunately, due to Amos's intensive networking over the previous years, the Swift band leader was also a friend, and offered him the role if he wanted it. Needless to say, Amos accepted.

For the past eight years, Amos has been touring the world as bassist for Swift, playing arenas and amphitheaters, which feels lightyears from his days as a bass-playing barista gobbling up gigs in small bars and casinos. On any given night, you are likely to pass the caravan of Swift buses, with Amos on board, speeding toward their next sold-out arena show. He has even developed quite a following of his own, amassing a large fan base among Swift devotees.

When he reflects back on the trajectory of his career, Amos points to that moment in the bar when his friend challenged him to get very specific about his aspirations as a key turning point. He said that if he'd not had a unique "calling card," he might not have been able to effectively navigate the complex and competitive channels of the Nashville scene. The key was making a choice and defining his unique offering.

BEING UNIQUE MEANS COMMITTING TO A PATH

If you try to be effective at everything, you will be effective at nothing. You must choose a path. This is the first and most significant responsibility of any creative professional, and it's the origin of all unique, authentic voices. The word *decision* is sourced in the word that means "to cut off." To decide is to fully embrace one option and cut off all others. This requires bravery, because each decision you make necessarily closes other doors.

Many people are afraid to commit to a specific course of action with their work because of a fear of missing out on other opportunities. The net result is that by refusing to choose a specific path, they are choosing for their work and their message to be middle-of-the-road and watered down. You will never develop an authentic voice unless you fully embrace what makes you unique and pursue it boldly. This requires that you have the bravery to decide between equally viable options, even knowing that you're risking making a bad choice. It's the willingness to commit that will ultimately set you apart. You have to own it.

However, you cannot arbitrarily choose a path. You must discern the most effective path based upon your own passions, skills, and experiences, and grow in your understanding of yourself and your aptitudes as you go about your work. This understanding will develop over time, and you must be brave enough to embrace risk even when there is little immediate payoff for your efforts.

TO BE UNIQUE, STEP OUT ON A BRANCH

Last fall I received an enigmatic text from a friend in Chicago that simply stated, "Dude . . . DJ Z-Trip is reading your book." According to my friend, who is one of his fans, Z-Trip posted a photo of *The Accidental Creative* on the Web along with some comments. I politely thanked my friend for letting me know, and went on with my life. About a month later, I was watching the Grammy Awards on television, and the closing number featured LL Cool J, Travis Barker on drums, Chuck D (of Public Enemy fame), Tom Morello (of Rage Against the Machine) on guitar, and behind them all, with a giant banner proclaiming his name, a man on the DJ turntables named Z-Trip.

Impressed with the performance, I grabbed my phone and casually sent a word of congratulations over the Web, thinking I would probably never hear back. To my surprise, Z-Trip responded quickly, and we began an interaction that eventually led to my attending one of the concerts on his summer tour with rapper LL Cool J. Standing in the wings, looking out over twelve thousand people bouncing and screaming in unison, was a fun and inspiring experience, and led me to wonder about how precisely a DJ forges such a unique style and earns a rabid following. As it turns out, Z-Trip's journey is a perfect example of how an authentic voice is rooted in a sense of identity, and cultivated through decisive action over time.

Z-Trip, whose real name is Zach Sciacca, told me his parents divorced when he was young. His mother went to live in Phoenix, while his father stayed in New York. As a teenager, living part-time in two very different cities exposed him to a wide range of cultural and musical influences. "When I was in New York I would get to hear all kinds of early hip-hop music. It was the really underground kind of stuff, and I thought it was great. Then I would go back to Arizona, and all of my friends there would be really into rock, but had no exposure at all to hip-hop, so I would share it with them and try to show them how great it was."

Sciacca recalls being deeply inspired when he first heard music producer and record executive Rick Rubin's early experiments in the 1980s combining rock and hip-hop styles into a single music track. Those experiments catapulted acts such as the Beastie Boys to the top of the charts, and put Run-D.M.C.'s collaboration with Aerosmith on the smash hit "Walk This Way" into the cultural mainstream. He told me, "I remember the first time I heard that and I thought, Yes! That's it! Somebody else gets it."

When Sciacca began taking small, early gigs as a DJ, he wanted to bring his love and knowledge of many musical styles to his audience, but at first he found that audiences were less than willing to venture outside their musical silos. The rock and rollers hung around only with others who loved that genre, and the hip-hop lovers spent time only with one another. "At parties, I was kind of like a bridge. I would mash up all of these different styles that I loved and introduce my friends to new kinds of music they'd never really been exposed to."

This bridging eventually became Sciacca's trademark. Over time, his skill and knowledge of diverse musical genres grew, and those early, skeptical audiences became raving fans. At first they didn't get it, because it was so original, but over time, Sciacca won them over by staying true to his vision. Now operating under the name Z-Trip, he became known as one of the godfathers of the "mashup movement," which centered around taking seemingly unrelated genres and mixing them together into a single composition. He became so successful, in fact, that others began mimicking his style. As he continued to grow as an artist, he began to branch out into using even more diverse and unexpected inspirations for his music, always trying to surprise his audiences, but still working to bring these seemingly disconnected influences together into something new and fresh. Whether playing for thousands of fans at a club or tens of thousands at a festival, Z-Trip said that he sees the journey of continually developing his voice as a central priority.

"I see growth as an artist being a lot like climbing a tree," he told me. "Let's say that the trunk of the tree represents your influences, because it has grown from your roots. You start climbing by staying close to your influences. However, at some point you have to choose to go out on a branch, and use your influences as support for a new form of expression. You have to go so far out on that branch that others are afraid to follow you, because it seems too risky for them. That's when you know you're in the company of one."

I asked him about the riskiness of engaging in this kind of behavior, because the farther out you go on the branch, the more likely it will break and you'll fall to the ground.

"Yes," he agreed, "but when you fall, it's like dropping a seed. That's when a new tree is created. That's when others start copying you."

As we saw in chapter 3, all people with unique voices begin as the product of their influences. They weave together those influences into something new that deviates from what's expected, and that creates a new kind of expression. They may begin by hugging the tree trunk, but at some point they choose to take risks with their work by making bold decisions. When they do this, they step out onto a branch, and begin following their own path. However, the one thing that keeps people hugging the tree trunk instead of taking risks is that they are afraid of choosing the wrong branch, or taking the wrong risk, and wasting an opportunity or appearing foolish. Like Z-Trip, you have to forgo the temptation to stay close to the middle and be willing to venture out onto a branch if you want to develop your authentic voice. It is only out on a limb that you will truly be in the company of one.

FINDING YOUR BRANCH

Before the start of each school year, our school district holds meetings in which teachers help parents better acclimate to the expectations of the teacher and to ask questions about the curriculum. This year, our second grader's teacher started out the reading portion of the meeting by sharing that the students will be using several "mentor texts." She said that these are books that give the students ideas about how they might want to shape their own stories and voice as they write throughout the course of the year.

While I'd never heard the phrase *mentor texts* used before, it's easy to identify several that have had a significant impact on my thinking and writing. From spiritual writers like Thomas Merton to business thinkers like Tom Peters, there have been a handful of "virtual mentors" who have defined my work and subsequently become a part of the way I think and share ideas. I go back to them over and over again, and in rereading them I always seem to find fresh insights.

Mentor texts don't have to be books, of course. It might be best to call them mentor works, because you may find inspiration for your work in film, interviews, sculpture, or music. Identifying your mentor works is a wonderful way to identify streams of ideas that resonate. They are the works of others that have most influenced your own.

Take a few minutes to do the following exercise:

Identify five important works that have shaped your thinking. Again, they can be in any form, but the important consideration is that they have inspired you in significant ways in your work. Which five works, experiences, or literal mentors have shaped how you approach your own work?

As you examine each of these mentor works, consider what it is about them that inspires you. Is it the ideas within them? Which ideas specifically? Is it the tone? If so, how? Is it the structure or the arc of the work? Try to get specific as you consider what most stands out about them.

Next, consider how these works have influenced your own work. What are the commonalities between your mentor works and your own work? Can you distill it down to a handful of qualities? Where do you see echoes of your mentors in your work? How so?

Finally, consider the differences between the mentor works and your own. Where have you diverged from your heroes and forged your own path? In what ways have you successfully pushed out onto your own branch and differentiated yourself from your mentors? Identifying the differences can be helpful in revealing some of the ways in which your perspective is different from that of those you admire, and some of the unique qualities you bring to the marketplace of ideas.

Now, as you examine the answers to these questions, consider how they might help you make bold decisions as you shape your future work. Where do you feel the need to further define your own voice so that it is unique from your influences? Where is your intuition leading you to take risks, even though it might mean stepping out onto a thin branch?

As your voice matures, it's easy to forget about those who have deeply inspired you, but returning to your roots is often an effective way to help you identify a path forward. It's possible for your work to become unnecessarily complex over time, and tracing a single thread back to its origin can help you parse through the noise and get to the heart of your resonant message.

FIND A SHERPA TO HELP YOU NAVIGATE THE BRANCHES

"I ran into someone the other day I took flying a long time ago," my friend Larry told me over coffee. "He said he still remembers rolling down the runway, and how I told him, 'Put your hands on the yoke, and just rest them there. Feel the moment when the wings come alive.' I don't remember ever saying that, but he said it's stuck with him for decades."

Though we never went flying, Larry played a similar role in my life. I was introduced to him at a point when I was exploring many questions about life and work for the first time, and I was told that Larry had thought deeply about these and many other issues. His passion was coffee, and he was a champion of a concept called the third place, which is the term for a location other than home or work in which social interaction is fostered and creativity emerges. Larry had forged his own third-place concept in a forsaken century-and-a-half-old church building informally dubbed "Old St. George," where he served amazing coffee and surrounded visitors with thousands of books on any conceivable topic. Larry and I began meeting regularly at Old St. George, and after a time he invited me to his home, where we would sit chatting and drinking espresso on his back patio every Thursday before work. The walls of his first floor and basement were lined with layers of books, and those that wouldn't fit on the shelves were stacked on tables or crammed into every available crevice. At some point in every conversation, when we got to a particularly deep part, Larry would excuse himself and disappear for the better part of five minutes, then reappear with a book on the precise topic we'd been discussing for me to take home and read before our next meeting. He even inscribed a few books with instructions and underlined passages and told me to keep them for my own library. Larry was the first person I could accurately tag as a "book bully," a phrase my friend Ben coined to describe someone who is constantly shoving books into the hands of others. However, he always seemed to know the exact book to point me to at just the right time to inspire my own risky exploration of my voice.

If I'd not met Larry, it's difficult to believe I'd be on the path I am on today. As I was climbing the mountain in order to seek answers to my deepest questions, Larry was the sherpa securing the line, showing me the footholds, and ensuring that I wasn't veering off course. He not only helped me find answers but also helped me ask the right questions.

This is the distinct difference between a traditional mentor and a more hands-on, sherpalike relationship. A mentor can offer advice without consequence. They may feel vested out of kinship or camaraderie, but in the end they don't suffer much if their advice doesn't pan out. A sherpa, on the other hand, is fully vested in the outcome. They aren't just tossing nuggets of wisdom at you, they are with you on the journey. Your success is theirs, as is your failure. In this case, Larry knew that I would be back the following week to hold him accountable to his recommendations. He was invested.

Here are a few truths about sherpa relationships:

They will be informal. Most of the people I've encountered who have reported having a sherpalike mentor didn't engage in a formal process to find them. The best way to find one is to simply look around you at people you already have a relationship with, and ask them for their very specific advice on a decision you're trying to make. Ask them for a resource or a book that they think might be able to help you. Ask them what is inspiring them. You will be surprised at how many people are willing to share. (Recall how Amos Heller asked a peer for advice on breaking into the music business. This was an informal, though highly valuable sherpalike relationship, as he gave Amos specific direction for his next steps. It takes humility to seek out someone for specific advice, but it illuminates your path toward growth.)

They will be seasonal. If you are open and seeking them, you will encounter many opportunities to engage in these kinds of informal sherpa relationships over time. There have been several people who have played a role similar to Larry's in my life, and in different areas of pursuit. However, these relationships didn't endure forever in this mode. They typically formed during a time of transition or challenge in order to help me navigate dangerous passes effectively, then transformed into something else. Don't feel the need to stretch them out into something unsustainable.

They will be mutual. There were also ways in which I was able to help Larry think through life and work, and in turn share my own thoughts and resources with him. We each brought our strengths to the table and helped each other gain clarity. To this day, I still occasionally help Larry with his writing projects and help him better organize how he shares his work.

Relationships are crucial to the process of uncovering your authentic voice. You need others to tell you what they see in you, to fuel the fire, and to open you to sources of inspiration and helpful resources that aren't currently in your field of view. You need kindred spirits who can occasionally evoke unexpected thoughts and help you refine your point of view so that you can make bold decisions with your work.

TO CODIFY UNIQUENESS, IDENTIFY YOUR PILLARS

You discover what makes you unique not by thinking alone but by thinking through action. As you interact with others through your work, patterns begin to emerge in how they respond to it, which leaves clues to the areas in which you are most effective. Remember that your voice is not just what you say but what others hear. You need to look outside yourself to see how your work is actually—and uniquely—impacting others.

That sentiment is echoed by Peter, who has been in real estate for about eight years. During that time, he'd experienced moderate and steady growth in his business, but had a difficult time finding a true "sweet spot" in the market. "The problem is that there are so many real estate agents, and there is so much noise out there, that it's truly challenging to differentiate yourself." Peter said he tried to use his inherent strengths to win new business, but most of what he originally tried was just too similar to what others were already doing. "I would approach potential clients, and their first question was 'What makes you different?' I didn't really have a satisfactory answer to that, because everything I said could also be said about nearly every other agent out there."

About three years ago, Peter became so busy that it was time to bring in a small team to help him. He realized, though, that he couldn't simply bring others into the business until he got really clear about the issues of uniqueness and voice. "Whatever issues I had regarding lack of clarity would only be magnified once I brought others into the mix." He decided to seek help from some friends with creative and branding experience, which led him on a process of self-discovery and to a deeper sense of purpose and identity in his work.

"They really challenged me to go deep," he said. "They were asking me a lot of questions about who I was, and what I really cared about, and at first I was tossing out a lot of phrases and words that didn't mean much. Again, they could have been describing anyone. However, they pushed me to look to my client feedback to help me understand who I really was." For years, after each engagement Peter had sent a client survey with two questions: "What went really well?" and "What could have been better?" While he'd read each and every survey, he'd never thought about seeking patterns and looking for clues about what made him different from the competition. "I was sitting on a gold mine and didn't even know it," he told me.

After poring over the survey responses, a clear pattern emerged, and was distilled into three distinct elements of Peter's unique identity. "Over and over again three things came up: calm, comfortable, and empowered. People said that I had been a calming force during the turbulent period of buying or selling a house, that I'd made them feel comfortable with the process and at home in meetings and show-ings, and that I empowered them with information and visibility into the process. Once I saw that, it was like a forehead-smack moment. It was so obvious to me that this was core to who I'd been all along."

Peter said that this deeper understanding of his identity has helped him prioritize decisions and vet potential opportunities. "A lot of people chase every kind of business they can find, but now I feel much more comfortable doing the things I know I can succeed at, because they are second nature to me. By focusing more deeply in con-nection with who I now know myself to be, I am growing my business more meaningfully and successfully."

Peter said that the exercise was like a rite of passage from childhood into adulthood for him. "Before the exercise I was like an undeclared college student. I was in college, and I was getting an education, but I hadn't really determined what I wanted to do yet. I was uncomfortable when challenged about why I was different. I was relying on some corny elevator speech that everyone told me to make, but it wasn't really true to my identity. It wasn't coming from a place of confidence because it was fabricated. What I know now is that everything has to flow from identity." In other words, Peter had chosen his branch and was stepping out onto it, taking risks with his work and trying to be true to his sense of identity and intuition. He was developing a unique, authentic voice by applying what he knew to be true about himself in his everyday interactions with clients.

Have you ever been through an exercise similar to Peter's? It can be powerful and help you to focus deeply on the areas that make you unique. However, to do it you will need a little help from your peers.

1. Identify five to seven people you've worked closely with over time, and who have seen you operate under pressure and at your best.
2. Ask them to give you three words that describe how they see you functioning when you are adding your greatest value, and a brief description of why each of the three is significant.
3. Ask, "What should I do more of, and what should I do less of?"
4. Ask, "If you were to sum up my unique value in a sentence, what would it be?"

Doing a survey of peers will not give you immediate, airtight answers, but it might give you a few data points to help you establish your pillars and better focus your efforts in a unique way.

RUNNING YOUR RACE

A runner friend of mine once told me that the most important mind-set principle for success in competitive running, especially in endurance races, is to stay focused on the ground immediately in front of you. In her opinion, many runners get suckered into expending too much energy too early in the race by less-experienced runners who dart out to the front of the pack due to race-time adrenaline. There is always a fear, she said, that the lead will become insurmountable and that the race is being lost. Because of this, some runners violate their game plan and try to keep pace with the front of the pack. Inevitably, she said, those runners slow their pace as they reach the limit of their training, and fall back to the middle of the pack. However, the runners who are wise enough to stick with their plan, forged by their months or years of training, inevitably rise through the ranks and finish near the front.

I've often thought about her insights when approaching my own work. It's tempting to look around at others who are doing similar work, and to allow what I see to cause me to violate my game plan, my pace, my strategy. It's easy to allow the plague of expectation escalation to cause my work in the immediate term to feel inadequate, even though it's simply in-process.

The lesson that I've embraced over the past decade of life and work is a simple one: because of unique passions, skills, experiences, and opportunities, each of us has a unique race to run. It's ours alone, and cannot be compared to the race being run by others. When we allow the stigma of judgment, comparison, or envy to tempt us off course, we violate the fullness of the contribution of which we are capable. We exhaust ourselves chasing "ghost runners" and "phantom success." We lose sight of the end goal, and in turn we lose sight of ourselves.

Many organizations I've worked with have succumbed to the very same temptation. Their strategy suddenly seems thoroughly unsatisfying when they see the gains being made by a competitor. As such, they begin to do things that are out of character, pushing themselves into territory that stretches everyone to the breaking point. Inevitably, there is the crash, the burn, and the rebuilding, all because they were suckered into chasing someone else's perceived success. (I've come to learn that the very things we envy are often well-constructed illusions, designed to inspire respect, but ultimately hollow in reality.)

Pursue uniqueness with your voice. Run your race. Execute your plan. Do your work, not someone else's. Don't allow envy, spite, ego, or greed to derail you or cause you to chase a phantom ideal that was never meant for you. You have a valuable contribution to make in the arena of influence you've been given, and a unique voice to offer the world, but if you are not diligent you may wind up gaining quick ground in the short term, only to watch the pack pass you a few miles down the road.

As artists, businesspeople, writers, and those desiring to create value in the world, it's easy to become consumed with fear of those who would tear our work down. We hear the voices of future critics in our head, and they can sometimes drown out the voice of our own intuition. As a result, we lose our bearing. You can't navigate from an illusory compass, but that's exactly what you are doing when you navigate your work from the place of trying to please critics. You are not creating your work for critics. Cynics will never come over to your point of view, no matter how eloquent your arguments and how beautiful your art. You cannot please them, so it should never be your aim to do so. Instead, you must have the courage to follow your intuition, to embrace your sense of identity, to do the thing that you are wired to do, and to grow into your voice, even in the face of criticism and bitterness. When one piece of work is met with derision and snark, put another in its place. When critics take apart something you care deeply about, keep building it and striving to find your audience. Remember that "everyone" is not the audience for your work, and if you fail to pursue uniqueness, you may never find your audience at all.

It takes bravery to know your strengths and to diligently operate within them. Be brave today, and run your race.

CHECKPOINT

When the phrase "find your voice" is used, it often means identifying what you care about that fuels your passion. Certainly there are elements of this, but it doesn't capture the totality of the concept. To find your voice means to identify the intersection of the value that you have to offer, your existing worldview and sense of purpose, and the true needs of the marketplace. It's about more than just what you care about or what excites you. It's about the unique way you are positioned to influence others and achieve impact through your work, which often begins by noticing how others respond to you. The following questions will help you explore your unique offering.

EXCAVATION

Did anything surprise you as you did the mentor works exercise above? (If you haven't done it, go back and think it through.) Are there any influences that you'd forgotten about, but that were formative in your development? (Sometimes as we grow, we even become a bit embarrassed of our early influences. However, they are still an important part of our growth and our voice.)

OBSERVATION

As you examined the areas where you diverge from your mentors and influences, what distinguishes you the most? How can you leverage that in order to set you apart from others in your field? What seems to be the through-line in your most effective work?

Are there any projects coming up over the next few weeks or months that might afford you the opportunity to step out onto a branch? How might you take a few strategic risks with your work to begin to define your uniqueness and reinforce what sets you apart within your sphere of influence?

REDIRECTION

How can you apply your knowledge of what makes you unique in your work this week? Consider how you might weave those themes through your conversations, the work you create, and the way you lead others. It's through applying uniqueness—acting upon what you know—that you will begin to distinguish yourself and define your "branch."

Chapter 5

Vision: Where Are You Going?

Vision animates, inspires, and transforms purpose into
action.

—Warren Bennis

Principle: For your voice to resonate, your vision must center on the audience you are trying to impact.

While it's important to turn your thoughts inward and reflect on what's
important to you, that's only the beginning of the process of developing
your voice. It's also essential that you turn your attention outward in
order to determine the kind of impact you want your voice to have on
those you serve. You must refine your vision for your work. While you
will never know exactly where your work will lead you, a guiding vision
will help you make crucial decisions and invest yourself in ways that
matter.

Often a vision for your work develops over time, not all at once.

Seth Goldman, cofounder of Honest Tea, told me that the first time the idea for the business arose he simply wasn't ready. "The idea for Honest Tea started way back in 1995 when I was at the Yale School of Management. My professor Barry Nalebuff was teaching a case study on the beverage industry. We were looking at the beverage shelves and Barry said, 'Is there anything that's missing?' My hand shot up and I said, 'Yeah—there are all these sweet drinks and all of these watery drinks, but there's nothing in the middle,'" Goldman told me.

Nalebuff told Goldman that they should start that very business, and encouraged him to start making samples and think about how they might be able to secure distribution. "I told him no. It just wasn't right at the time. It wasn't until a few years later, when I was in New York City and went for a run, and I went to a beverage cooler for something to drink, that I realized, 'Wait, there's still something missing on the shelf.' That's when I reached out to Barry and said, 'I'm ready to do something about this now.'"

Goldman and Nalebuff set about launching a low-calorie product that would taste great but be made from tea leaves and organic sweeteners. There were no organic tea drinks available at the time. "If anything, we were a little ahead of our time when the company finally launched in 1998. We were bringing out drinks that were around seventeen calories when the rest of the market was at one hundred calories. The only places we succeeded initially were the natural-food stores, because most people just weren't ready for a drink like that."

Since that time, Honest Tea has grown from start-up to selling more than 100 million bottles per year.

"We didn't have any of the advantages of the larger companies we were competing against. Our only advantage, really, was that we had something different."

Goldman told me that muscle and distribution alone are not sufficient to guarantee that you'll achieve critical mass with your idea. Just because you make something, he said, doesn't mean that people are going to beat a path to your door. "You have to have something different. You can't just be a 'me too' product. The shelves are full. You have to justify your place."

In his opinion the most important quality for an entrepreneur is to be fully vested in a vision. "You have to build something you're passionate about. The world is too competitive and life is too short. If you're not one hundred percent in on all fronts, it's just too easy to get knocked down and not get back up." This doesn't mean that you have to enjoy every aspect of what you do, but that you have to have a compelling vision that continues to push you forward even when things get hard or obstacles materialize in your path. You have to understand the space you're trying to occupy, and the change you're trying to create.

"From the beginning it's got to be something you're passionate about. If you care about it in a way that's in the fiber of your being, you'll run through walls, you'll do those hard things. You won't lose your resilience. Obviously, the fact that I'm still here after we sold the company proves it's still something important and something I believe in. When the Coca-Cola Company bought Honest Tea in 2011 people said, 'What are you going to be doing?' and I said, 'What do you mean?' It's always been my goal to build this into something big and something important. Seventeen years later I still feel like we're just getting started."

At the entrance to Honest Tea headquarters hangs a sign displaying a Chinese proverb: "Those who say it cannot be done should not interrupt the people doing it."

A vision helps you understand the effect you want your voice to have on your audience; it will give you the drive to keep going when the work itself gets difficult. To channel your work toward a compelling vision and develop your authentic voice, you need two things: a precise focus on whom you are trying to reach, and an empathetic understanding of how you want to influence them.

ATTRACTING YOUR AUDIENCE

The lights dim, and the screaming begins. Thousands of people wait in anticipation, many of whom have spent several hundred dollars just for the privilege of being in this room for the next ninety minutes. Then, in the darkness, a small, unmistakable sound begins and the crowd explodes. Just when it seems the roar can't get any louder, a spotlight illuminates a figure in the front of the stage, and complete pandemonium ensues. It's easy to get swept up in the excitement, both for the performer and for the crowd. Even though I spent much of my early adult life in bands performing for large crowds, I still get lost in the moment at concerts, not because I'm enthralled by the presence of one of my favorite performers but because of the promise of what's about to happen. There is a gift exchange that will take place between the performer and the audience. The performer shares a gift with the audience, and the audience reciprocates.

This scene plays out thousands of times each night around the world, as bands take the stage to play to their adoring fans. There is an almost sacred bond between artist and fan that has been earned over time through the precise, intentional shaping of a body of work. When fans spend money to go to a show, they know generally what to expect from the band. Though the set list and staging may change, they know that the band isn't suddenly going to appear onstage and play a completely new genre, let alone to act out a Shakespearean play or begin lecturing on particle physics. Bands know that they have earned their fans by developing a recognizable voice, and that the fans are there to experience the magic of live music. It's an unspoken deal.

The same deal is made when buyers stand in line to purchase the latest novel by their favorite author, when a client approaches a favorite designer about a new freelance project, or when a manager asks a top employee to speak at an upcoming company-wide meeting. In each of these scenarios, there are ingoing expectations based upon past performance, and the degree to which you meet those expectations will determine success or failure in the eyes of the audience. If you waffle and violate those expectations too often, you are unlikely to forge a raving long-lasting fan base.

Precision is an important factor in gaining a loyal audience for your work, and it's also one of the more difficult things to accomplish. Precision doesn't mean that you operate by rote or always do what is expected, but it does mean that you are intentional about how the value you consistently deliver stays true to a through-line you've established for your body of work. If you are not diligent about this, it's easy to give your potential audience whiplash as they try to keep up with you. Over time, they will stop paying attention altogether. Your vision for your work is the glue that holds your experimentation, development, and expression together. It's what defines the shape your voice takes.

This chapter is the most granular and tactical of any in this book, but it's that way for a reason. Honing your voice with precision requires getting into the weeds and hacking away at what doesn't belong. Remember, brilliant, resonant voices are shaped with great effort over time.

CLARITY AMID UNCERTAINTY

True clarity is rare. In truth, clarity can be intimidating because it requires commitment. It can be much more comfortable to be noncommittal because you are less polarizing that way. It's tempting to become imprecise and unclear in your work so that you can cover all the bases. However, while this is a natural reaction, it's the opposite of what you must do in order to create impact. To hone your voice so that it's sharp you must understand who you are trying to reach, and who you're not. You must define your intended audience.

Several decades ago, a term was coined to describe the ability of content creators to reach more precise, though smaller markets with content specifically tailored to their interests: narrowcasting. Originally, it was envisioned that narrowcasting would be conducted through the more traditional media of satellite and cable television, and the explosion of niche cable networks in the 1980s and 1990s proved this idea correct. However, over the past decade, narrowcasting has become ubiquitous, as the Web has allowed anyone with an idea or interest to connect with like-minded tribes. Unlike broadcasting, which is by definition about spreading an idea far and wide, narrowcasting is about delivering precise, targeted messages to a specific audience at a time of optimal effectiveness.

Contrary to the world of broadcasting, which primarily focuses on capturing the largest audience possible with its message, and waters down the message in order to make it widely palatable, narrowcasting is often most effective when it is polarizing. By sending precise signals about who is "in" and who is "out," a narrowcaster can create a more fanatical audience and increase the likelihood of engagement with an idea.

Here's the problem: at scale, narrowcasting requires bravery. It seems much more safe to scatter your message broadly with the hope of capturing an audience, but the new landscape of communication often punishes unknown voices who try to be too general. When you try to reach everyone, you may unfortunately reach too few. However, if you focus on deeply resonating with a specific segment of the potential audience, you may find that your message spreads much more effectively.

HAVING A VISION MEANS SAYING "IT'S NOT FOR YOU"

One of my favorite things about speaking at conferences is that I always leave challenged by the other speakers and by hallway conversations with the conference participants. At a recent event, one of my favorite sessions was an open Q&A with entrepreneur and author

Seth Godin. He said something I'd heard him say before, but for some reason it really resonated this time:

"As soon as you're willing to say 'It's not for you,' you're freed up to make art."

Translation: not everything you make will be for everybody, nor should it be. Even more to the point, if you are trying to make something that's for everybody, then you are probably compromising your art, which means you are sacrificing great possibility on the altar of immediate pragmatism.

One reason this happens, as mentioned in chapter 2, is a fear of critique. When you're first sharing your work with the world, critique stings. You have very few data points by which to judge whether or not your work is reaching and impacting its intended audience. However, as you share more broadly over long periods of time, you begin to see patterns emerging within groups of people who resonate with your work, those who don't, and those who are indifferent. (As your voice becomes more refined, the indifferent crowd typically grows smaller.) The key is to be willing to listen to critics and incorporate valuable feedback without allowing their comments to stall your progress and growth.

Remember that it's easier to tear something down than to build something new. Despite the sense of personal empowerment people feel when they critique someone else's hard work, no one ever changed the world by lobbing a witty critique from the cheap seats. If you want to create impact, you have to enter the arena. As Brené Brown wrote bluntly, "If you're not in the arena also getting your ass kicked, I am not interested in your feedback."

In those areas where you have discretion over the kind of value you create, have the courage to follow your instincts, to take risks, and to stand up for your work. If you want to see something change, then make something to replace it.

THE JIMI HENDRIX / MONKEES EXPERIENCE

Did you know that Jimi Hendrix once toured as the opening act for The Monkees? It's a little funny to consider in retrospect, given their relative individual influence on the generations of musicians that followed, but for the tour promoter it made sense at the time. Hendrix was a newcomer to the music scene, and while he was a daring and celebrated underground artist, his platform had not yet matured in proportion to his voice. Mickey Dolenz, a member of The Monkees, saw Hendrix perform in New York, and when it came time for the band to kick off their tour he strongly pushed for the talented guitarist to get the opening gig. Hendrix's management perceived the move as an opportunity to get him onstage in front of thousands of potential new fans. The Monkees, on the other hand, had a massive platform due to their much-hyped television program, which had stoked the flames of fandom for teen girls everywhere. (The band was originally formed solely as an ensemble for the show, and only later became an actual, touring band.) Though they'd released a few singles and were very popular, they weren't taken seriously as a band by music insiders. They were desperate for industry credibility, which was one reason that Hendrix was considered to be a good fit. They were hoping to appeal to a different, more mature audience.

As you'd probably suspect, the experiment didn't last long. The teenage-girl fan base of The Monkees was visibly dismayed by Hendrix's guitar antics. At one show, when Hendrix attempted to get the crowd to sing the lyrics to "Foxy Lady," they instead insisted on singing "Foxy Davy" as a tribute to Davy Jones, the lead singer of The Monkees. As the legend goes, only a handful of shows into the tour, Hendrix became so frustrated with the crowd in the middle of a set that he waved a profane gesture, threw down his guitar, and stormed offstage. Stories like this, of mismatched touring artists, are abundant. There are other disastrous examples, such as The Who opening for Herman's Hermits, or Bruce Springsteen opening for Anne Murray. We all know in retrospect that Jimi Hendrix eventually found a loyal audience and went on to make music history, but if you were a Monkees fan in 1967, you might have thought you were witnessing a career implosion.

When you define your audience and boldly pursue precise, clear work, it is not going to be for everyone, and you have to grow comfortable with some people disliking it. In fact, I will go so far as to say that if you don't experience any degree of friction, you may not be taking enough risks. The worst, least productive thing you can do is to contort in order to try to fit the expectations of an audience you don't care to reach anyway. You may get a lot of attention, but you will not ultimately achieve impact.

YOUR INTENDED AUDIENCE

The most important method for refining your vision is to closely and specifically define your intended audience. Getting specific about how you target your work may mean that it will take you more time to grow your audience, but in the end you will have a more loyal fan base. For any piece of work you create, you need to know who it is and isn't intended for as you strive to stay true to your vision.

As you create something, here are a few principles that will help you precisely define your intended audience (IA):

Whenever possible, think of a specific person. Who is the one individual who perfectly epitomizes the reason you're creating the work? If there was one person who would most benefit from what you're making, who would it be? Craft your work for that person.

When I was writing my first two books, I kept the name of a specific person—my intended audience—next to my laptop or in my notebook, where I would see it often. Whenever I began to lose my bearings, I would pause and think about my intended audience and consider how I would explain the concept if they were sitting across the table from me. Even now, when I get stuck, I stop to consider the person I'm writing for, why it will be important to them, and how they will best receive the information I'm delivering.

Many companies use a similar process for defining their intended customer or audience. They call this imaginary person their avatar, and aspire to create products and marketing messages that will resonate with them. Some even go so far as to name the imaginary person and refer to them often in conversation, as if they were real. ("How would 'Bob' like this?" or "What would 'Susan' think?") However, as you consider your personal work, I'd encourage you to identify a specific, real person you are aiming to reach because it will keep your intended audience from becoming too abstract and impersonal.

Don't fall into the trap of creating for a group or demographic; this results in generic work. Your voice will naturally spread if it is precise and resonates with your intended audience.

Think impact and resonance, not immediate results. Stay focused primarily on the outcome you're trying to achieve with your work, and center all of your efforts around it. Focus on the value you are trying to add to the life of your IA first, and you are likely to create something that they will want to consume and share with others. One certain way to fail to achieve your desired impact is to make your IA feel like the target of a strategy or the object of a marketing plan. If you create something for your IA, they should feel like it was made for them personally. What do you want for them? How will they be different for having experienced your work? Be as concrete as possible.

Don't change IAs midstream, and if you do, start over. Sometimes you may discover in the midst of making something that you were wrong about your IA from the start. When this happens, don't just adjust your message and continue to plow ahead. Instead, stop, go back to the beginning, and think about the work through the lens of your new IA. It might mean starting over, or scrapping a significant amount of work, but if you don't take this step, then it's likely that your finished product will feel watered down and imprecise.

Consider a piece of work that you are creating. It might be a new initiative within your organization, a draft of a novel hidden in your desk drawer, or a marketing plan for a new product you're launching. Regardless, try to answer the following questions:

Who is my IA for this work?

What outcome (impact) am I trying to achieve for them?

What expectations will they have of me when they experience this work, and how can I meet and surpass them?

How might I surprise and delight them by overdelivering in unexpected ways?

As counterintuitive as it seems, you are better off with a small, highly targeted audience of raving fans than a larger audience that is lukewarm to your work.

IMPACT BEGINS WITH EMPATHY

As a child of the 1980s, my after-school hours were often filled with sitcoms and syndicated reruns of the popular television programs of the previous decades. Most of these shows had catchy theme songs, some of which—much to my chagrin—I can still sing word for word to this day. A few of the most catchy theme songs were for shows created by legendary television icon Sherwood Schwartz. For example, the entire context for his show *Gilligan's Island*, which is about a group of unlikely shipmates who encounter a storm during their three-hour tour and wind up stranded on a deserted island, is painted in the opening theme. Another of Schwartz's shows, *The Brady Bunch*, begins with a ditty that explains how an unlikely group became a family, and sets the audience up for what they're about to see.

While he was often ridiculed for the overly explanatory theme songs, Schwartz had a very specific reason for why he chose them. He was once asked why he felt the need to explain the entire backstory for his shows in the intro to every episode.

His reply? "Confused people don't laugh."

Schwartz understood that if new viewers lacked context for the show, then they were unlikely to get as much enjoyment from it, and were therefore much less likely to become regular viewers. By bringing everyone up to speed with each episode, he was able to ensure that no one felt like an "outsider," and thus create an inviting viewing experience.

These same principles apply regardless of the kind of work you do. It's important to provide context for others, and to help them understand the flow of the story so that they can more easily assimilate new information. We understand new stimuli in our environment by comparing it to past experiences and determining how it fits the existing patterns and mental constructs we hold about the world and how it functions. If you are diligent about helping people understand the context for your work, then you are requiring less effort on their part to understand and apply it.

The first step in your ability to provide context is empathy. It's not the responsibility of your intended audience to adapt to you, it's your responsibility to adapt your idea so they can receive it.

The word *communicate* is derived from the Latin word *communis*, which means "common." The roots of the word imply that it's about making something common through sharing it with others. This is contrary to how we often think of communication today. In an age in which everyone has a platform, to communicate often means to blast a message out to the masses.

I'd challenge you to ask "What am I trying to make common? What feeling, idea, insight, or breakthrough has taken root in me that I hope to inspire in others as well?" In order to build this bridge, you must get inside the aspirations, fears, and struggles of your audience. You must cultivate an empathetic worldview. Few people question any longer the true value of empathy from a marketplace perspective. In fact, many people and companies have realized that empathy is not only a "nice to have" quality in work but an essential one. In his book *The Empathic Civilization*, Jeremy Rikfin argues that the race to become more empathic is essential to our survival as a planet. "The constant empathic feedback is the social glue that makes possible increasingly complex societies. Without empathy it would be impossible to even imagine a social life and the organization of society." Empathy, he argues, is the key to societal progress. I believe that it's also the foundation of creating authentic work that resonates with others.

BUILDING COMMON GROUND

In 1985, a young musician took the stage at Colby College in Maine to entertain local students. The event was reportedly organized as a morale booster for the community, after several incidents involving teens. The seventeen-year-old hip-hop artist began his set by proclaiming "Now, what you're about to see right now is known as rappin' and scratchin'." He went on to explain in great detail what a DJ is, how "scratching" works, and how the music is constructed for a live set. The entire scene, which was captured on video and is still available online, shows that while the audience was appreciative, they were less than sold on the music. Still, it was an impressive effort, and it demonstrated the kind of empathy often lacking when an artist shares a new art form with an audience. The artist, LL Cool J, was only months away from the release of his first album, *Radio*, through which he achieved massive success and was catapulted into the upper echelon of the music business. However, I think that this early video speaks volumes about his desire to build a bridge with his audience. Many artists would have simply jumped onstage, performed their set, and shrugged it off when the audience didn't get it. Instead, by centering on the needs of the audience (not his own), LL Cool J was able to create common ground.

SEEK is an innovation consultancy that, in the words of CEO Jerry Haselmayer, aspires to "humanize innovation for the world." According to Haselmayer, they work with large brands and causes to help them "return to who they really are," and ultimately enable them to reach others through empathic innovation. "Empathy ultimately leads to empathic ideas and products, because when you experience empathy you are centering your efforts on the person you are serving," Haselmayer told me. "Deep down, I think there is a human desire for connectedness. We want to be engaged, trusted, and in touch. The troubling thing is that we are not often taught how to do that, so we approach problems at a distance, without any true sense of connectedness to the person for whom we're solving the problem."

Though empathy seems like a high concept, there are practical ways to cultivate it and apply it to your work. Geoff Zoeckler, a SEEK employee who has spent significant time exploring the impact of empathy in the workplace, believes that empathy has three unique parts: head, heart, and gut. "You sometimes see something, and it has an emotional impact on you, but it's often left there," he said. "To experience empathy, you have to move on to the next stage, which is that of compelling action. Otherwise it's just sympathy, not empathy."

With sympathy, Haselmayer explained to me, you feel something for the other person, but you are detached. With empathy, you cross the line into compulsion. You feel that you must act. "Saying 'that sucks' is sympathy, but when that shifts to 'this sucks' it means that you are vested in it and ready to act," Zoeckler added. "It's not a simple task, it requires a tremendous amount of energy. The emotional state of others becomes a part of you, and you are now vested in the results. It starts with a choice to engage empathically and the willingness to actually act on what you feel."

According to Zoeckler, there is a four-part process to acting with empathy: decide, identify, recall, act.

To decide, we have to suspend our prejudgments and willingly choose to make the empathic connection. "The reality is that we all interpret things through our own filters. Thus, we must first make a decision that we will identify with the other person. This decision sends a signal to our mind that it's necessary to associate what the other person is experiencing with our own memories and emotions." The moment we decide to feel empathy for the other person, we move from a passive connection to a more active one.

The second step is to actually begin to identify with the feelings or needs of the other person. "It's not 'Oh, my father passed away too, so I understand you.' It's about actually feeling the emotion the other person is feeling. It might be the time you lost a job or the time you experienced another type of loss, but the important thing is to actually feel the emotion of the other person." This is the key difference between sympathy and empathy. You are actually feeling something akin to what the other person is feeling in the moment.

Next, you recall that specific experience, and you consider what your needs and wants were in that situation. Because you are closely recalling your own needs at that time, you can start to more precisely identify what the needs and wants of the other person might be. As this process unfolds, it creates a compelling desire to help solve the problem alongside them.

Finally, you act on your compulsion in the way you believe will best serve the other person. Because you have been through the entire process, your actions are much more likely to be in-line with the true needs of the person you are serving with your work. "You must see this process through to the end. You can't manipulate based upon partial visibility into the data. It must honor the individual," Zoeckler warned.

The potential for manipulation is something that concerns him, because once emotions are involved it becomes easier to influence others to do what you want. "To manipulate is to poke and prod without true empathy. It's acting to achieve a result without having been through the emotional experience. We won't allow clients into the ideation session unless they had a genuine emotional connection with clients at the beginning of the project."

Empathy requires vulnerability, which involves risk. A bit of sacrifice is required to connect empathically and create work that resonates deeply with your audience. However, empathy is not a sign of weakness, it's a sign of strength. It is a strong, confident response to circumstances.

Haselmayer explained to me that his drive to fuse empathy and innovation was in large part sourced in a traumatic childhood experience. "When I was young, my father and I helped a friend's family build an aboveground swimming pool. There was a ladder to get into the pool, and my father slipped on it and broke his neck. He was immediately paralyzed, and became a quadriplegic. The doctor told him that he would likely have only six to eight years to live, because without the ability to move around he would eventually lose his muscle and would develop bed sores that would grow worse and kill him."

Haselmayer paused, and I could tell that just recalling the scene still evoked strong emotions. "My father could have given up, but instead he dedicated himself to figuring out a solution to the problem. He invented a mattress system that kept him off his back thirty percent of the time. He's now been living as a quadriplegic for forty-six years, something the doctors said was nearly impossible. My father was inventing stuff, but not because of some business objective or the desire to make money. It was about survival in the purest sense. Because of this, I have seen firsthand how life changing innovation can be. Innovation is not abstract to me, it's personal. It's deeply human." His vision for helping others innovate was rooted in his own early experience of how innovation can make life more humane and meaningful.

I believe that you will find it challenging to be an effective leader, manager, or creator if you lack empathy for your audience. It is the origin of lasting impact through your work, and bedrock for developing an authentic voice. In order to express yourself in a way that resonates, you must first be able to feel what it's like to walk in the shoes of your intended audience.

What does your intended audience need, want, feel, fear, and hope for? What do they expect from you, and how can you not only meet those expectations but surpass them by filling an unspoken need or want? Remember that your work is not about you, it's about the impact you create and the value you deliver to those you serve. This all begins with an empathetic vision.

MAKING "THEM" THE HERO

Because we have different experiences and perceptions of the world, we could look at the same set of facts and come away with very different conclusions. A great illustration of this is the antismoking ads funded and created by United States tobacco companies in the early 2000s. The ads came out of a 1998 settlement between forty-eight states and four tobacco companies, and were supposedly designed to encourage teens to stop smoking (or never start). The typical ad featured a sincere, fatherlike figure sharing statistics about the dangers of smoking, and exhorting them to shun the habit until they were of age. Some of the ads told teens that if they faced any pressure at all from their peers to smoke they should let their parents know. As the ad reminded them, their parents were on their team.

From the outside, these ads seemed to do everything that was required in the settlement. There was a strong message about the dangers of cigarettes, an appeal to shun negative peer pressure, and even a suggested course of action in the event that peer pressure was overwhelming. The message was "Think. Don't Smoke."

But when the data came back, analysts were a bit surprised to discover that the pattern of teen smoking had not changed much during the period the ads ran. Far from being the effective industry-funded anti-smoking tool they'd wanted it to be, the government had actually funded ads that appeared to have achieved the opposite result.

Compare this with the truth ad campaign, which was the only non–tobacco-industry-led campaign launched as a result of the settlement. Also created with the intent of curbing teen smoking, the ads took a much different tact. They typically featured some overt public act of protest, staged at the entrance to a tobacco company corporate headquarters. Statistics were shared about the effects of smoking on health and longevity, and the tactics tobacco companies allegedly used to gain new customers. Finally, there was a call to action for teens that involved standing up for truth and refusing to allow these corporations to trick them into become unwitting participants in their corporate ploys.

The results? Far different from the industry-funded ads. Because the person delivering the message in the truth ads was typically a peer, there was more of an empathetic connection with the audience. The public protests were far more attention grabbing for teens than stats and dramatic role play. But there was a final element that really sealed the deal for the truth ads. They tapped into sentiment that was already very much present among teens, and has been for centuries: the need to define yourself by defying authority.

Smoking had historically been seen as a means of rebelling against the expectations of society and being your "own person." Many teens started smoking in order to be "cool" or to be seen as a rebel. However, by turning the tables, the truth campaign was able to show teens that, far from being an act of rebellion, smoking might actually be exactly what "the authority" wanted them to do, even if it was against the teens' own best interests. In other words, they were being tricked, and the curtain was finally being pulled back. The challenge? Stand up for justice and refuse to cooperate with their scheme. Fight back against the machine. Be a hero.

In the years in which the truth campaign ran, teen smoking dropped precipitously. Prior to its launch, the annual smoking decline among teens was around 3 percent. In the first few years of the truth campaign, it was 7 percent. According to a 2002 study published in the *American Journal of Public Health*, "Exposure to the 'truth' campaign also appears to have changed the way youths think about tobacco. The percentage of youths who held anti-tobacco attitudes and beliefs increased by an amount that ranged from 6.6% to 26.4% during the first 10 months of the campaign." While there were certainly other factors involved in these results, the numbers show that the ads resonated deeply with teens because they had crafted the message from a place of empathy. The campaign reflected the deeper needs and desires of the audience, and its messaging was designed to tap into the inherent need for identity and belonging felt by adolescents worldwide.

Question: As you consider your work, how can you use your under-standing of the needs and desires of your audience to put them in the posi-tion of "hero"? How can you shape your ideas with empathy so that it's obvious to others that you are trying to enlist them in something great?

THE EMPATHETIC EPIPHANY

The offices of Epipheo, a video production and marketing company, are located inside historic Longworth Hall just west of downtown Cincinnati, Ohio. The company originally occupied one modest clus-ter of offices, then two adjacent ones, then half the floor, and now parts of two floors of the two-city-blocks-long building. Their explosive growth is the result of their uncanny ability to distill their clients' message into a three-minute video, and share it in a way that resonates with the customer.

Epipheo was founded in 2009 when video artist Jon Collins created a short clip to promote a movement called Advent Conspiracy, which attempted to challenge the shopping habits of consumers during the Christmas holiday season, and the video went viral, attracting millions of views in a short time. Convinced there was a potential business to be found in creating similar videos for companies, Collins enlisted the help of three friends who eventually became the founding partners. "We were trying to figure out what was so powerful about that initial video, and what made it spread so quickly," Jeremy Pryor, one of the founders, told me. "We realized that at the heart of it, we'd delivered an epiphany to the viewer—something that reframed the viewer's perspective—through a short video. Thus, epiphany plus video became 'Epipheo.'"

One of the first videos Epipheo created was a short explanation of a product launched by Google in 2009 called Google Wave. After a long demonstration by execs at Google's I/O event, many were still left a bit confused about what exactly the product did. While many understood that it was supposed to help with collaboration and communication, the demonstration was so involved and complex that it left many people scratching their heads. Within a week of the event, Epipheo crafted a short video called "What Is Google Wave?" and published it to YouTube as an experiment. The video quickly garnered hundreds of thousands of views and was featured in several major media outlets, which certainly reinforced the partners' belief that there was value in their idea. However, the real proof of their business model arrived within a few days, when Google unexpectedly contacted Epipheo to inquire about creating videos for more of its products, such as AdWords and Chrome OS. Shortly after those videos hit the Internet, clients such as Facebook, Yelp, Microsoft, Mercedes-Benz, and dozens more were knocking on Epipheo's door inquiring about videos of their own.

"The real challenge of what we do," explained Pryor, "is that we aspire to fundamentally change someone's perspective on a topic in just a few minutes' time, which means that we truly have to distill our message down into its key elements." The constraint of two to three minutes of screen time forces you to consider the best possible way to deliver the true meaning of the message. "Creating short-form videos also lowers the bar of engagement for new ideas, which means that it's more likely people will invest the time to hear them out, versus having to invest hours in reading a book or listening to a lecture." The epiphany itself is a gateway to a breakthrough in thinking about a topic, which can then lead to further action on the part of the person experiencing it. Thus, it quickly became apparent to the founding partners that the key to their business was in their ability to get to the core idea—the true meaning—as quickly as possible, which isn't always as easy as it sounds.

"Sometimes we hit a hurdle because of the curse of knowledge," Pryor told me. "The person on the company side has sometimes invested months or years of their life into getting this product just right, so they want to point out all of the nuances, design details, and technical specifications to make sure that none of it is lost on the audience. The problem is that the audience doesn't care about features and benefits until they understand why the product is important in the first place. What problem does it solve? Why should it matter to me?"

What Epipheo discovered is corroborated by research into the science of memory making. People tend to remember important events long after they've past, but not all events find equal footing. What matters most in forming long-term memories is the personal meaning that we ascribe to the events, and thus how intertwined they are with our sense of identity, desire, and purpose, and not simply what transpires. Regardless of how memorable an event might seem at the time, if there is no personal "hook" involved to help us assimilate the memory, then we are likely to forget it over time. It's the story that we tell ourselves about what happened—whether or not we are conscious of it—that causes certain events to stick. For this reason, it's often the case that our understanding of the world can become a self-reinforcing system, sometimes full of assumptions and false causation. This is why an epiphany, especially when delivered in a short format with a lot of visual cues, is so powerful. It instantly calls into question unchallenged assumptions and long-held beliefs that could be preventing the audience from achieving its goals, and thus has instant personal meaning.

The hardest part of getting to the epiphany, however, is getting inside the life and mind of the audience. This is where Epipheo has a distinct advantage over their clients, because their outsider position allows them to approach a topic with fresh eyes. This means it's easier to view the problem and solution as a potential customer might. As Pryor added, "Who's having the epiphany? The audience member. Therefore, they are the hero in the story. We share a common problem or misconception they are likely to have, then we walk them through the story of how it's been solved, and, most important, why that solution has meaning. When it works well, the audience member comes away thinking 'Now that I've experienced this epiphany, I can't go back to the way things were before.'" They are changed in some way because of the sudden insight.

The added advantage is that those who experience the epiphany tend to become the most ardent fans of the idea. Thus, the videos—and the impact—tend to spread quickly and broadly, with some of them achieving millions of views in just days. The best ideas take on a life of their own.

Can you remember a time when you suddenly realized that a long-held assumption was invalid, or that an understanding you had of the world was patently false? It's likely that you can remember in vivid detail where that epiphany occurred, how it was delivered, and how it changed your thinking on the topic. The human mind is wired for predicting the future based upon existing patterns of understanding. This is the only way that our minds are capable of maintaining order in the midst of the bombardment of information that flows at us each second of the day. When one of those existing patterns is challenged, and a new piece of information is introduced that interrupts the predictability of your environment, your mind goes on high alert and forms a new neural connection. When that connection triggers enough existing neural networks to form a new systemic pattern of understanding, an epiphany occurs. This can be a large epiphany ("Unicorns don't actually exist") or a relatively minor one ("My manager hates getting bad news by e-mail"), but either way it's a new understanding that reframes your perspective.

"We're always asking how we can elevate the story into something that inspires the viewer," Pryor concluded. "Apple always said that they wanted users to fall in love with their products, which I thought was ridiculous until I switched to using one, and then I felt for the first time what he meant. My irrational love of my laptop made me a better writer, and it bled over into all of my work. That's the kind of epiphany-inspired action we hope to cultivate through how we tell our stories."

Question: As you consider your vision for your work, what is the epiphany that it is designed to inspire? How are you changing the minds of your audience so that they will never be the same again?

Ultimately, crafting an epiphany for your intended audience is an act of empathy.

EVOKE, DON'T PROVOKE

One of my most poignant memories of childhood is of Matthew, the elementary school bully. Due to his being held back a few grades, he dwarfed everyone else in the class, both in height and in girth. Every day at recess he would plant himself in the same spot, just to the right of the slide, harassing people on their way down.

Every so often, someone would muster the courage to confront Matthew and his bullying ways. When this happened, a bloodthirsty crowd would encircle the pair hoping for a fight—an actual fistfight. After a long stare down, Matthew would—like a cliché from a TV show—reach out with his foot and draw a line in the mulch, muttering some variant of "I dare you to cross this line." Often the challenger would come to his senses and simply walk away while his nose was still intact. However, occasionally someone would show Matthew that he meant business, and would push him until he reached his limit. A fight would commence, typically broken up by a playground monitor before there was a clear winner, and we would all go back to playing basketball or tag.

While few of us have to deal with real-life bullies like Matthew any longer, the bullying ethic is still alive and well. I often think of Matthew when I encounter an idea that is designed to provoke a response in me, or manipulate me to act in the moment, or robs me of my time and attention in order to force me to take notice of someone else's agenda. I often feel the same way as when Matthew would draw the line on the playground with his foot and challenge us to cross it. Everything centers around the agenda of the bully, which is all about getting attention. It's about being provocative, and doing it at the expense of others.

To provoke means to stimulate someone to respond. It means putting a finger in their chest and picking a fight, or pushing their buttons until they have to do something about it. A provocation is a challenge to act, whether that means throwing a punch or clicking a link.

A lot of emotion-laden messages are provocative. They are designed to elicit a desired reaction, but often with little concern about what will happen after the moment of response. They are designed for instant gratification.

By contrast, to evoke means to call something forth from the other person. When you are evocative, you are causing something to surface in the mind of the other person that will inspire them to action and cause a change of perspective. It is designed for permanent rather than temporary effect.

Provocation is a selfish act, because it's centered around the needs of the person communicating. The only consideration is to get the other person to perform as desired, whether or not it's in their best interest to do so. Evocation is a generous act because it recognizes that the best way to inspire lasting impact is by calling out the best qualities of the other person and presenting them with a free choice about what to do.

Provocation is self-centered; evocation is others-centered.

Provocation is a temporal fix; evocation is a permanent shift.

Provocation is fear or scarcity based; evocation is rooted in generosity.

Provocation says "You'd better do this, or else . . ."; evocation says "We must do this, because . . ."

Provocation dies when its end is achieved; evocation lives on through the changed lives of others.

As you consider your message, it's worth asking yourself whether you are operating from a place of provocation or evocation.

Ultimately, empathy is about cultivating a deep understanding of your audience, and working hard to craft your expression so that it is contextualized for them. Is your work tuned in to the needs of your audience, or is it tone-deaf? Are you creating from a position of serving others, or of self-service?

If you want to influence someone to see something from your perspective, you must understand that pointing them to the facts of the situation will never suffice. You must instead become a curator of experiences and information so that you selectively weave a story that guides the other person to your point of view. This is not manipulating the facts, it's wisely presenting them in such a way that the other person can relate to them. It's what a photographer does when framing a shot, or a sculptor does when eliminating the unnecessary parts of the stone. They are, in a way, curating the experience of the end user such that their unique point of view will be evident.

You are the curator of your own work, and the shepherd of your own point of view. It is not the responsibility of the audience to move toward you, it is your responsibility to move toward them, welcoming them into your world.

As you connect deeply with the needs and desires of your intended audience, your vision for your work will be refined, and the best path for connecting with them will be illuminated. Remember that vision is about "Where am I going?" and as a part of that, you must consider "How will I take others with me?"

CHECKPOINT

When developing Vision for your work, it's easy to become too "safe" as you're trying to deliver on the expectations of your audience. The key is to learn to deliver upon expectations while continuing to push into uncomfortable places and forge new avenues of thought and work. It's a tricky balance, but one that you must strike if you want your work to be remarkable.

EXCAVATION

Consider your recent work. Is there anything that you are doing repeatedly right now that is out of character for you? Is there any part of the way you engage your work that is inconsistent with how you want your work to be projected to your intended audience?

Can you think of examples of your work that are especially empathetic, in that they seem to really connect deeply with your true needs? What are they, and what makes them especially resonant? Can you think of times when you've created work that seemed to penetrate deeply and connect with your intended audience? What made that work especially effective and resonant?

OBSERVATION

What can you prune from your work to make it more precise and consistent? What needs to go away so that your work can have a more consonant tone?

In general, who is the intended audience for your work? Put yourself in their position for a moment, and consider how they might describe your work in a sentence. Does it reflect how you'd want them to describe what you do? If not, what would you hope they would say instead?

Consider work that you are currently in the midst of. What are three words that describe the needs of your intended audience? How can you better shape your work to make it connect more deeply, based upon these needs?

REDIRECTION

As you consider your in-process work, make certain that you have a specific intended audience. If not, define your intended audience, then check to see if there is anything you are doing that is inconsistent with what will resonate with that audience.

This week, practice going through the four-step process (decide, identify, recall, act) before engaging in a conversation or sharing an idea. Try to approach each interaction or piece of work from the perspective of your intended audience.

Chapter 6

Mastery: How Will You Get There?

> The future belongs to those who learn more skills and
> combine them in creative ways.
>
> —Robert Greene

Principle: To develop a voice that resonates, you must gain mastery over the basic skills necessary to express your ideas and over emerging themes in your environment.

A strong grounding in your identity and a clarifying vision for your work are both important, but to develop an authentic and compelling voice, you must also master a set of skills that lets you bring that vision into the world. There are two categories of skills that we'll focus on in this chapter. The first is the refinement of your basic craft, which gives you the leverage you need to express your idea. The second is an intuitive mastery over emerging ideas and themes in the world around you, and your ability to contextualize your work in such a way that it will be accessible to others.

WHERE PREPARATION MEETS OPPORTUNITY

In 2013, music legend Billy Joel was giving a combined lecture and concert at Vanderbilt University in Nashville. During a Q&A session, a young man stepped up to the microphone and boldly asked "the piano man" if he might accompany him on his classic hit "New York State of Mind," prompting a roar from the audience. Joel agreed, and invited the young man (named Michael Pollack) to the stage. When Joel asked which instrument Pollack planned to play, the reply was piano, prompting another response from the audience. It was pretty gutsy to take over Joel's instrument on one of his iconic songs.

Joel then asked Pollack which key he wanted to perform in, to which he replied, "Any key you want." After working through the logistics, the two broke into an astounding rendition of the song, which featured several vamps by each performer and a few instrumental breaks for Pollack. At the end, the duet earned a standing ovation, and as the young man made his way back to his seat, an obviously impressed Joel proclaimed, "Remember that name, Michael Pollack!"

Pollack went on to do several media interviews about the event, in which he stated that he'd been a longtime fan of Joel's music, and that he'd been learning and practicing his songs for more than eight years. He and his friends had planned the question when they heard that Joel was going to be in town, but they hadn't planned on the video of the event catching fire through social media like it did.

Here's what I find interesting about this example: there were likely other pianists in the auditorium that evening, and perhaps even some who were more accomplished than Pollack. However, only one had prepared for that moment and saw it as an opportunity to utilize his skills in a once-in-a-lifetime way. There is a lot of naysaying in our culture today about the importance of "being picked" by the powers that be, and encouragement to "pick yourself" and go out and make things happen without permission from others. While I agree whole-heartedly with the sentiment behind these encouragements, the pur-pose of picking yourself is so that you can put yourself squarely in the place where your work will eventually be noticed and given an even broader audience by those who are capable of doing so. In order to increase the likelihood of this, you must (a) be in game shape at all times, and (b) learn to spot emerging ideas and opportunities.

MASTER YOUR DAYS TO STAY IN "GAME SHAPE"

I was recently on Coronado Island, near San Diego, California. The ride from the airport to the resort passed through a narrow strip of land that housed a naval base on one side, and the barracks and U.S. Navy SEALs training facility on the other. As we passed, I saw several SEAL recruits out on an obstacle course, climbing ropes, and running the beach. My driver, who had a friend who was once stationed there, said that their presence on the beach is near constant, and that they're frequently out there all night training and staying "battle ready." I liked that phrase. It means that even in times of relative quiet, when there are no obvious deployments on the horizon, they were required to stay in the kind of shape necessary for success in the event that they were called upon to perform a mission.

I've often heard a similar sentiment expressed by athletes. They talk about the importance of being in game shape, meaning that they are ready at a moment's notice to jump into a game and perform well. In the off-season, they will often express their desire to stay in game shape through regular workouts and a specific training regimen. By the time the season arrives, they have done the necessary work to maintain their endurance, muscle tone, diet, and even mind-set so that they are sharp and up to the challenge.

What does it mean for you to stay in game shape? Frankly, many people I've met are barely getting by in their work, and always shooting from the hip rather than making investments in their ability to perform when it counts most. However, those who consistently perform at the highest levels recognize the urgency of their work and do their best to maintain rhythms that help them persist in excelling.

What are some examples of practices that help you stay in game shape?

> Immersing yourself in the great work of your industry, and studying the thoughts and patterns of its leaders.

> Regularly engaging in conversations with peers and people you respect about what is inspiring them, then working those resources into your own well of inspirational stimuli.

> Getting enough sleep to allow your mind to assimilate information and your body to restore itself.

> Eating properly so that your brain has enough of the right kinds of nutrition, and you have stamina and energy to spare.

> Saying no to really good opportunities so that you can focus your time, energy, and other resources on the work that you know is most important.

> Clarifying the challenges you are trying to solve through your work so that you have a razor-sharp understanding of where you are headed.

You know that opportunities will arise at some point, and in order to take advantage of them (and time your work well) you must do the difficult work along the way so that you are ready.

As you consider the work for which you are accountable, what should you be doing daily to ensure that you will be able to deliver at a moment's notice, when the timing is right? What does it mean for you to be battle ready?

SLOW AND STEADY DOES NOT WIN THE RACE

How many times have you heard the phrase "Slow and steady wins the race" trumpeted as a recipe for success? As you probably know, it comes from the fable about a race between a tortoise and a hare. The race is an obvious mismatch, as anyone can see. Because of his blazing speed, the hare makes occasional pit stops along the course, believing that he can always make up his lost time later in the race and still win. The tortoise, on the other hand, believes that persistence is his most valuable tool, and he keeps up a steady pace throughout. The hubris of the hare is his downfall, and the tortoise eventually crosses the finish line victorious because of the consistency of his effort.

Over time, this fable (and its corresponding moral) has been parroted by managers, writers, and consultants exhorting listeners that "slow and steady" is more important than raw talent.

The problem? While in essence it's a solid principle, the way it's applied is often more harmful than helpful. Slow and steady definitely do not win the race alone. Slow, steady, and deliberate win the race, when punctuated by occasional sprints.

It's not enough to make daily, measured progress on your work if it's not deliberate progress. If you're not moving in a meaningful direction, then failure is a likely outcome. To develop your voice, you must determine the skills that you must master, and set aside time each day for developing them, which means deliberately pushing into uncomfortable places and stretching your abilities. Recall Joshua Foer's comment about how many people get stuck in the OK Plateau and never push beyond it. To develop your ability to deliver your work in a way that resonates, you must be sharp.

Define what meaningful progress means today:

What problem are you working on? (Not what project, or what tasks, but what problem.) Make sure that your deliberate practice is flowing up into an outcome, not just keeping you busy.

Be clear and vocal about expectations and objectives:

Ensure that you and your collaborators understand one another's expectations for the work, your individual roles, and the deliverables. One way that "slow and steady" gets off the rails quickly is when everyone is moving in slightly different directions. At first this may not be noticeable, but over time these slight differences of understanding become large and visible gaps in progress.

Fail forward:

Yes, it's a cliché, but it's true and important. If you are going to take purposeful risks and thus potentially fail, make certain that you are failing in a meaningful way. Fall in the direction of your objective, not to the side. Always strive to understand the potential obstacles and pitfalls of your actions, and consider ahead of time what you hope to learn if your attempts fail. You will often miss what you're not looking for.

Practice deliberately:

One of the most misunderstood and misapplied examples of the slow-and-steady principle is the touted "10,000-hour rule" that emerged from the work of K. Anders Ericsson but was largely popularized by Malcolm Gladwell in his book *Outliers*. Many people share the principle as indicating that one can "become world-class at anything by doing it for 10,000 hours." This is simply untrue, and not an accurate reflection of the original research. More accurately, someone with a natural aptitude who dedicates 10,000 hours of deliberate practice to a specific kind of activity or field can become very accomplished. However, no matter how many hours I jam with my garage band, we are unlikely to become The Beatles. What you have to do is dedicate yourself to deliberate practice, meaning that you break down your bigger objectives and tasks into smaller skills and then work purposefully to develop them over time. (In *Die Empty* I illustrated this process by prescribing step, sprint, and stretch goals.)

Be ready to sprint:

On occasion, growth requires a sprint. While your slow, steady, deliberate progress will be enough to get you moving in the right direction, you also have to be prepared for those moments when the work will demand everything you have for a season. This is not (necessarily) unhealthy if it's a part of a natural rhythm, or ebb and flow, of your work. However, if it's something that happens every week, it means that you are likely headed toward burnout. Sprint when necessary, but if you are being intentional and deliberate, your work should require occasional sprints, not an all-out footrace.

Don't be lulled into the idea that being busy and making progress is necessarily going to net you a win. You have to be intentional and deliberate about your activity, and you have to be willing to sprint when the occasion calls for it. One way to structure this kind of deliberate, voice-shaping activity into your rhythms is a practice I call the dailies.

PRACTICE EVERY DAY WITH THE DAILIES

To ensure that you are always in game shape, and to develop your skills and voice daily, it's helpful to establish a set of regular practices that help you sharpen and develop necessary skills.

A great example of how ritual and repetition can lead to progress is the structure of life in a monastery. For centuries, many monks have abided by strict adherence to a set of practices they call dailies. While the specific activities vary from situation to situation and monk to monk, the dailies are comprised of a set group of chores, vigils, prayer or meditation times, and sacramental rituals. Regardless of the day, regardless of external circumstances, and regardless of their motivation, the monks will engage in these dailies as an act of devotion to their cause.

For many years, I've practiced something very similar in my life and work. There is a set number of dailies that I've incorporated into my routine, and at the end of the month I will check to see how consistently I performed on them and whether or not I am behaving consistently with my objectives. This is my method of deliberate practice.

I created an index-card-sized spreadsheet, then in the left-hand column I listed my daily rituals, and in the top column I put a number for each day of the month. I keep the card in my notebook for daily review, and whenever I perform one of the dailies I check it off for the day.

My dailies are all related to specific long-term goals that I want to achieve in life or work, and are designed to keep me on track mentally, physically, emotionally, and spiritually. For example:

PERSONAL DAILIES

Read for sixty minutes. Every day, this is the first thing I do. If you look at the records of my dailies, you will find very few unchecked boxes here, and when there are it's typically due to extreme circumstances like sickness or hectic travel. To sharpen my thinking, and to ensure that I have a good sense of what's going on in the world, it's important for me to have dedicated time on a daily basis to filling my well with new thoughts, the perspectives of others, and creative inspiration. This is a key way in which I immerse myself in mentor works and hone my creative instincts.

Write one thousand words. This is how I engage in deliberate practice of my craft. A writer writes, and I know that if I want to continue to have ideas and be able to turn phrases, I need to stay in game shape. This means that I write at least a thousand words a day, regardless of whether I have a big project to keep me moving forward. Sometimes these words find their way into my work, and sometimes they are simply exploratory in nature and designed to help me try out new styles and develop new writing skills.

Review objectives. I keep an index card in the back of my notebook with my big projects (and my big three open creative problems at the moment) and review them daily. I'm not setting specific actions for them when I review them, but only keeping them top of mind so that I don't go too long without meaningful progress. This helps me apply any themes that are emerging within my notables to my upcoming work.

Exercise. I tend to walk about five miles a day, and I have a very specific regimen I follow. (I often walk to a specific coffee shop about two and a half miles from our home, spend about a half hour writing, then walk home. Along the way, I'll listen to audiobooks or podcasts, though sometimes, if I'm working on a specific problem, I just use it as free thinking time.) This is a way that I get some movement in, and also interact with my mentor works to sharpen my intuition.

Talk with each child. I strive to have a meaningful conversation with each of our three children and with my wife every day. Fatherhood is a significant way in which my voice finds form.

Meditate/pray. I strive to take a significant pause each day to interrupt the madness and cull my thoughts. It's during this time that I "space out," free write, and allow my mind to wander, as discussed in chapter 4. Often I find new ideas and themes during this time that I'd previously overlooked.

BUSINESS DAILIES

Three ideas for content. Ideas are the lifeblood for any creative pro, so I try every day to come up with at least three new ideas based upon what I'm experiencing that I can share with others.

One business development activity. It's easy to let this one slip, but small activities can add up to a lot of business over time. Whether it's a call to a client, making an introduction, or writing a note to a colleague, this small activity helps me to keep forward momentum. This is a part of me refining my vision for my work and engaging to build my platform in a more meaningful manner.

One piece of content. I try to produce one piece of content each weekday. Most of them never see the light of day (because they're shared privately with clients or in my newsletter list), but the practice keeps me in shape and forces me to use my voice in novel ways.

Here's the thing: regardless of what your dailies entail—and I'm sure they'll be very different from mine—it's important that you have a set of practices that you come back to and that help you refine your skills and express your voice daily. They keep you moving forward, not just living with the illusion of progress (which is so easy to slip into). They help you develop your voice, because they force you to continue moving even when you want to stop.

If you go to toddhenry.com/dailies you can download a worksheet to help you develop your own set of daily practices.

Remember that it's not what you know that matters, it's what you do. Set your dailies, and stick to them, and you will be better positioned to take advantage of opportunities. Step by step and day by day, over time you will refine your skills and your perception, and you will be prepared to take advantage of opportunities as they arise.

MIND THE WAVES

A few years ago, while on vacation in Hawaii, my friend Darin and his son Tommy decided to learn how to surf. Being from Ohio, they don't get to the beach much and saw this as a once-in-a-blue-moon chance to ride the waves. After asking around, they were directed to a beach in Lahaina, where they were greeted by a man with the slightly unsettling nickname "Sharky." As Darin put it, "He had long, blond hair—imagine Prince Charming from *Shrek*—and he spoke to us with a lot of 'dudes' and 'brahs.' He was the stereotypical 'surfer dude.'" Sharky helped them gear up, and after a bit of instruction they were out in the water, frantically trying to catch the waves. After an hour or so, they grew tired and decided to call it a day. The next morning Tommy decided he wanted to spend the last day of their vacation surfing again, so the entire family went down to the beach to watch.

Tommy geared up and headed out into the ocean as the family stood next to Sharky, watching him ride a wave, paddle back out, and ride another. "He must be exhausted," Darin said to Sharky. "I'm sore from only an hour of surfing yesterday, and I can't imagine how he must feel being back out there again."

Sharky paused, then replied, "Well, the problem is that you guys don't know how to surf. You guys are trying to get all of your surfing in within just an hour or so. Real surfers will come out and be out there all day. It's not about being efficient, it's all about the experience of it and finding the right wave." He paused, then continued. "We may take only two or three waves all day long. You guys take two or three waves every ten minutes. It's not about squeezing it in, it's about choosing the right waves."

Darin told me that Sharky's words rang true about more than just surfing. He's learned to apply them to life and work as well. "Just like in surfing, there is an art to reading the waves. You have to be able to discern what's going on in the landscape and when the right time is to act. You must slow down enough to read what's happening around you, and make it part of your profession to separate the real opportunities from the false ones. Every wave looks the same to you until you learn to discern them. Every wave can look like the next big thing, but most of them just fizzle out."

It's all about timing. If you act frantically, trying to jump on every opportunity and ride every wave that looks promising, you'll only wear yourself out and miss the real opportunities. However, if you learn to time your work properly, then you can take advantage of already existing momentum to carry your message further and cause it to resound more deeply. As Ken Kragen, the successful talent manager and producer, once wrote, "You can do the best work in the world, but if the timing isn't right, it's going to be wasted."

You should be playing with a lot of ideas and maintaining a portfolio of activity, some risky and some more conservative. By doing so, you will be better prepared for the moment when you are thrust into the spotlight, and better equipped to make a strategic leap when the stars align.

MASTER EMERGING IDEAS

So far, we've mostly focused on two things: what you care about (identity), and what your audience cares about (vision). However, there is a third factor that you must consider if you want your voice to truly resonate: the context into which you introduce it. This means paying attention to ideas that are already gaining momentum, or opportunities that may provide external energy for your own work. The adoption curve will be much shorter if you are able to contextualize your work within something that's already familiar to your audience and has cultural momentum. This requires the skill of timing.

To be clear, this doesn't mean chasing trends or trying to "news-jack," a phrase popularized in the past several years to describe the tactic of jumping opportunistically on news stories in order to borrow some of the spotlight. Rather, it means doing a bit of extra work to understand what is already going on in the marketplace of ideas, and then contextualizing your idea so that there are existing "hooks" for your audience to hang it on. Whether you're trying to share a book or music or sell a new idea through to your client or manager, your voice will much more likely be heard if there is context for it.

Even if an idea is brilliant, it may not be accepted if the timing is wrong. Ron Jackson, professor of communications at the University of Cincinnati, told me that this third factor is often critical in determining whether or not an idea is accepted. "Everyone wants to be part of a winning team, so our natural inclination as human beings is to want to support success. We want to see Michael Jordan play the game, not someone who is missing all of their free throws. Once there is momentum behind something, people begin to see how they fit into it and they get on board."

Psychologists call this the bandwagon effect, meaning that people are more likely to become enthused about an idea when they see that others around them are also getting behind it. As history shows, this can be a dangerous phenomenon if used as the primary mechanism for decision making, because it sometimes causes you to arrive at premature conclusions based upon deceptive evidence. Not all popular ideas are good or valuable. However, understanding the human tendency to get behind something with momentum can also give a needed boost to your ideas, if you time them properly.

If you want your voice to resonate, then you must pay attention to valuable thematic patterns emerging in your environment. You may have a brilliant, world-altering idea, but if there is no context for it because the timing is off, then you will struggle to be heard. You have to contextualize your work for your audience. When you look for opportunities to use your voice at the intersection of these three factors (what you care about, what they care about, and emerging ideas), then you are giving your work its best possible chance to succeed.

#LIKEAGIRL

In July 2014, a short film caught fire via social media, filling news feeds and walls and garnering millions of shares and views. The film begins with a behind-the-scenes shot of a casting call, as a twenty-something actor steps into the light. "Hi, Erin!" a producer says. "Okay, I'm going to give you some actions to do, so just do the first thing that comes to mind. Show me what it looks like to run like a girl."

In stereotypical fashion, Erin proceeds to run with her arms flailing about, clearly more concerned about her looks than about her gait. The video then cuts to several more actors, both male and female, responding to the same command. Each person skips with their arms, legs, and hair swinging wildly in "girlish" fashion.

Next, the actors are told to "fight like a girl." They bat their hands in front of their faces like they are swatting away flies. Next, they are instructed to "throw like a girl." They each demonstrate a weak throw, acting exasperated with their inability to toss the ball very far.

The film next cuts to a ten-year-old girl named Dakota, who is also told to "run like a girl." She immediately starts running hard in place like she's competing in a race. Several other young girls follow suit. When told to fight "like a girl," they throw hard jabs. When another young girl is asked, "What does it mean to run like a girl?" she replies, "It means to run as fast as you can!"

The film then poses the question "When did doing something 'like a girl' become an insult?"

Since its release in June 2014, the three-minute film has been viewed more than eighty million times worldwide. It was sponsored by the Procter & Gamble feminine-care brand Always, and was produced by ad agency Leo Burnett, and an abridged version of the film was later aired during the 2015 Super Bowl.

I asked Edgar Sandoval, VP of Global Feminine Care for P&G and Always brand, why they chose to produce the film, and he told me that it was actually a continuation of work that has been ongoing for decades, though often beneath the radar. "We've been trying to champion the self-confidence of girls and women for thirty years. Each year we reach between seventeen and twenty million girls across sixty-five countries with our puberty education program, because we know it's a critical but also a confusing life stage for many girls," Sandoval told me. As the father of three girls, Sandoval said that the campaign was in many ways deeply personal as well. "Our research indicated that ninety percent of women surveyed said that words had damaged their self-confidence during puberty, and more than fifty percent of girls lose significant confidence during those same years." He said that the objective of the campaign was to "get to these girls before they are convinced by the world that to do something 'like a girl' is a slam."

Sandoval reached out to their ad agency, Leo Burnett. "They had a great team led by Judy John, and one of the key deliverables was to identify the voice of Always in the social space. They took on the task, and came back with the idea of the #LikeAGirl campaign as a social experiment." The end result of the experiment, however, was far from certain. "It was a completely candid film, so it was a risk—we didn't know exactly how people would act on camera."

John told me that as they were generating ideas for the campaign, the phrase "changing the meaning of 'like a girl'" was written by a team member on a single sheet of paper. "There was so much work up [on the walls] in the room, but as soon as someone said that phrase, there was an instant recognition that it was a really profound idea. It really touched everyone." John said that everyone had a story of how they had misused the phrase in a derogatory way. "I have a daughter, and I knew that I'd used that phrase before, and I remember thinking, I'll never say that again."

At the end of the film, the original adult actors are shown how the young girls responded when prompted to behave "like a girl," and they are clearly saddened by how they'd originally acted. When asked if they'd like another shot at acting "like a girl," they reply yes, bringing the film to an emotional crescendo with the statement "Let's make 'like a girl' mean amazing things."

While more than 95 percent of the response to the film has been positive, Sandoval said that there has also been some pointed criticism. With other, similar campaigns having achieved prominence over the past few years, such as Dove's "Campaign for Real Beauty" (which also featured messages of affirmation for women), some have suggested that Always is simply being opportunistic by creating something to play on the heartstrings of its audience. "One of the critiques we get is that we are jumping on the women-empowerment bandwagon. However, it's important that people remember that we've been doing this for thirty years! This is nothing new for us. It's the same message we've always championed, we're just finding a new outlet for it. We are able to reach people so much more effectively through social media than in other ways."

He continued, "This campaign was near and dear to my heart. It's something we'd been putting a lot of thought behind, and it's exceeded all of our ingoing expectations. It managed to accomplish the perfect fusion of what we care about and what the consumer cares about, but in a credible way." Some skeptics will always question whether a big business can truly care about the emotional needs of its consumers, or if it's simply a form of manipulation to increase loyalty, but Sandoval believes that it's not only possible but necessary for business to stand for more than only profit. "In order to help [raise the self-confidence of girls], we have to achieve financial goals and do good at the same time. These can both coexist, and they must."

When asked why he personally thought the film was shared so far and wide, Sandoval said, "I think what made it especially resonant is our desire to tell the truth in a very genuine manner. In order to be a trusted brand, you have to. And the film did this for the viewers in a very unexpected, surprising, and rewarding way, so much so that they felt compelled to share it with others."

The #LikeAGirl campaign is a near-perfect example of the confluence of those three major forces, discussed above, that work together when the timing for an idea is right: what you care about, what your audience cares about, and ideas that already have momentum. The Always team was concerned with increasing the confidence of girls and women while simultaneously building the value of its brand. The general audience was concerned with the perceived injustice of "like a girl" being used as an insult, and also with finding something inspiring to share with their friends and peers. Finally, the idea of empowering young girls and women to be confident in their abilities and appearance is an idea that has momentum, as had been seen in other recent cultural movements. Constructing a campaign at the intersection of these three forces was bound to have an explosive effect.

If you wish to be successful in causing your work to resound, you must account for each of the three confluent forces.

What do I care about? What are the resonant themes, the outcomes I'm committed to, and the tenets of my vision for my work? What is it I'm trying to create or change with my idea? What makes my message authentically mine, and unique? What change am I trying to introduce into the world of ideas?

What do they care about? What outcomes and themes does my audience hold dear? What do they want to see happen in their lives or in the world? What outcomes do they desire?

What ideas already have momentum? How can I connect my idea with something that is already charging forward and gaining cultural momentum? Can I rely on something else to provide context for my idea so that it speaks for itself? What are the "hooks" that will make my idea stick?

You will be best positioned to create impact once you can respond to these three questions and build your platform at the intersection of your responses. However, impact can rarely be fabricated out of the blue. You need to be working diligently and shaping your work so that you are poised to take advantage of opportunities when they arise.

FORM YOUR COLLECTIVE

One way to test your ideas and identify possible overlaps with ideas already gaining momentum is to spend time with others who are doing similar work, or who are at a similar life stage.

Several years ago, my friend Kevin Hern realized that since he graduated from business school, he was growing disconnected from the many conversations with classmates, professors, executives, and entrepreneurs that were a formative part of his experience there. He decided to create a weekend event in a centrally located city to reconnect with classmates and other peers who had sharpened him in his journey in order to share what they were learning, and to learn from people who were a little further down the path. The event was dubbed "Camp Hern," and has now been going strong for seven years. As a part of the weekend, Kevin invites mentors (which in years past has included business tycoons, ex-governors, spiritual leaders, etc.) to share their perspectives on current events, and then lead discussion groups about how these events should shape our thoughts and work. I've found these weekends valuable in helping me to process what's happening in the world, to generate ideas for my business and for my clients, and to build relationships that help me feel more connected to the pulse of culture.

While the weekend retreat is a wonderful format, it's not necessary to jet across the country in order to connect with peers. How could you set up a similar "collective" in your city?

Here are a few suggestions about how to do so:

Identify a handful of people who inspire you, or who you know will bring a measure of brilliant thinking to the table. Make sure that you are choosing people who will sharpen you and challenge you in some way to be better at what you do.

Set a time once a month (or bimonthly) to get together over coffee, or at a local restaurant or pub. The gathering should feel pretty informal. Make sure that you're meeting in a place that will be conducive to conversation, so not too noisy.

Choose a topic for the evening based upon current events, a trend in the marketplace, or a question related to life and work. Each person should know the topic in advance so that they can forge some initial thoughts and come prepared to discuss.

Have a set of questions prepared, but let the conversation go wherever it leads. You'll be surprised at how productive these conversations can be when allowed to take on a life of their own. Additionally, you'll be surprised at how many ideas and insights come from hearing how others process and respond within the conversation.

Over time, you'll find that the collective provides you with great context for ideas that are shaping the marketplace. Remember that the objective is simply to connect with others, share ideas, and process your thoughts together. The objective is not—nor should it ever be—to make this a "pitch session" or a problem-solving meetup.

Often the best way to create impact is to simply get your idea out into the marketplace, observe, then redirect as needed. However, by spending time with others, sharpening and refining your perspective, you may find that you are able to tap into themes that you'd previously overlooked.

If you want to achieve impact, you must commit to the mastery of your skills and an understanding of the ideas garnering the attention of your intended audience. As you achieve mastery, you will learn more about who you are (identity), and where you're going with your work (vision), and the cycle of growth will continue as you develop your authentic voice.

CHECKPOINT

Staying aligned and in touch with what's happening around you is a significant part of delivering great work in a timely way. However, as with anything, it can also be dangerous to both your personal growth and your ability to serve your audience if you become too driven by circumstance and ignore your own intuition while chasing trends. As such, it's critical to see timing as only one aspect of a resonant voice, and to recognize that it must also be aligned with the other elements of voice if you want to connect with your audience. Be prepared, stay diligent, and, as much as you can, remain in game shape so that you can jump on opportunities when they arise.

EXCAVATION

What are the basic skills of your craft that you need to develop so that you are better able to bring your ideas to the world?

As you survey the area in which you work, are there any ideas that seem to be emerging right now? Are any ideas gaining momentum that in some way connect with the work you're already doing?

OBSERVATION

What daily practices do you need to incorporate into your life so that you can stay in game shape? How can you work measured, daily practice into your routine?

How might you shape your work in such a way that it's taking advantage of those themes or emerging ideas? For example, is there a way in which you can make reference to those themes in your work as corroborating evidence or as a cultural touchpoint to generate a bit of extra momentum?

How much time do you spend connecting with others and getting in touch with what's happening in the culture?

REDIRECTION

Visit toddhenry.com/dailies to download the dailies worksheet and begin your daily regimen.

Make a list of five to seven people you'd like to connect with as a collective, and determine when and where you will meet with them. What will you discuss as it applies to your current work? What in-process work might you share with them in order to gain perspective and fresh insights about how to better shape it for resonance?

PART 3

Everyday Application

Chapter 7

Everyday Practices for Developing Your Voice

The virtue of a man ought to be measured not by his
extraordinary exertions, but by his everyday conduct.

—Blaise Pascal

Throughout the book you've become acquainted with how Identity,
Vision, and Mastery flow together to help you develop your authentic
voice. However, on a daily level, when work gets overwhelming and
you have a dozen paths in front of you, each of which seems valid, how
do you make decisions that are consistent and consonant? It's one
thing to understand these core drivers on a conceptual level, and it's
another altogether to apply them practically day to day as you shape
your authentic voice.

I use the word *shaping* intentionally, as the diligent development of your voice through your work is about making decisions,

refining your understanding, and chiseling away at everything that doesn't belong. You are like a sculptor carving away the block of excess stone until you release the sculpture within. This process begins by embracing the three core responsibilities that you must tackle each day.

THE THREE RESPONSIBILITIES

As a creative pro, you have three primary responsibilities. First, you have a responsibility to your stakeholders. These are your clients, your company, your family (because they have a stake in your success or failure), and anyone else who is depending on you to deliver. The significant challenge is that, when the pressure is on, it's easy to appease the people who hold the power of the purse strings, in whatever capacity that might be, and ignore your other responsibilities.

The second responsibility is to yourself. You have the core responsibility to listen to your intuition, to pursue your productive passion in the course of your work, and to add unique value. You must learn to follow your gut and take risks. You owe it to yourself to learn to hear the voice of your intuition. To some people this might sound a little frivolous or too "soft," but your skills of perception are greater than you probably give yourself credit for. It's just that your inner voice is drowned out by the external noise or the clamoring to appease your stakeholders.

The third responsibility—and stay with me here—is to the work itself. You have to ask yourself—and be willing to accept the answer to—"What does this idea want to become?" Each project has a life and trajectory of its own, and needs to be given space to become what it naturally wants to be. This sometimes means suspending your attachment to the ideas of your stakeholders and your own intuition and playing with the idea as it takes shape. You have to allow the idea to breathe, which sometimes means engaging in activity that is gloriously inefficient.

The struggle of developing your voice—and often the reason we get stuck—is due to the tension between these three responsibilities. If you are compromising your self-responsibility to appease your clients, you will lack motivation. If you are prematurely optimizing your work in order to shape it to your own intuition, you will either displease your clients or suffocate the work. Similarly, if you simply play and play with the idea, you may miss the mark entirely because you are being paid to do a job, not just experiment.

So, which of these do you personally struggle with? I think that I struggle most with the responsibility to myself. I'm more than willing to allow an idea to take shape, or to ensure that I'm meeting the needs of my client, but I often do so at the expense of my productive passion and my own intuition. I am going to establish a discipline in the coming year of taking time each day to better listen to my inner voice as it relates to my work.

In fact, I challenge you to do the same. Choose the one responsibility that you think you struggle with the most, and commit to a small daily act that will up your game in that area. For example:

If you struggle with responsibility to stakeholder,

> discipline yourself to seek the opinion of a stakeholder every day on an issue you normally wouldn't bring up with them;

> say "thank you" every time you receive feedback, even if you don't like it;

> write a note of gratitude once a week, and take ten minutes each day to think about why you are thankful for your clients, manager, peers, family, and other stakeholders.

If you struggle with responsibility to self,

> take fifteen minutes each morning to sit in silence and reflect on your priorities and your work. Pay attention to your inner dialogue;

> build a buffer into the middle of each day in which you reground yourself in silence before reengaging with your work;

> take a few minutes before you change tasks to pause, breathe, and think about what you're about to do;

> at the beginning of a project, consider how your productive passion will play a role in the shaping of your work.

If you struggle with responsibility to the work,

> build a few minutes into your day to play with ideas, even if they aren't relevant to your current project;

> put a note at your workstation that says "Follow the work" as a reminder to occasionally allow the work to lead the way.

In addition to these actions, you can analyze your work each day through the lens of Identity, Vision, and Mastery to ensure that you are charting a course of growth.

IDENTITY: KNOWING YOURSELF

Of the three drivers of authentic voice, the easiest to lose sight of in the course of your work is identity. As you strive to meet the demands of the marketplace, and to keep up with emerging ideas and trends, or even to chase after the skills you think will serve you well into the future, it's often the case that you lose connection with the very thing that animates your best work. You must remain rooted in why your work matters, and allow it to inform your daily choices.

The key is to make progress each day, and to not become overwhelmed with the size of the task. Long-arc goals are met by accomplishing a series of short-arc redirections, which means constantly realigning your work toward the magnetic poles of purpose and identity. I don't mean to sound overly simplistic, because it's certainly not easy to do so and you are unlikely to always know where your work is headed, but you are much more likely to do remarkable work if you have a decent understanding of why the work matters to you.

Below are some practical ways to begin refining your sense of identity and applying it to your daily work.

BREAK AWAY TO LISTEN

Having met many accomplished songwriters, authors, entrepreneurs, and artists, I've noticed that many of them use similar language when describing their creative process. They talk about "listening for the idea," as if it exists just beyond their grasp. They sense that something great is about to emerge, and they've seen the shadow of it, but haven't yet quite settled what it is. They work the idea in their mind until the brilliance emerges.

This kind of listening requires intentional time, focus, and dedication. I encourage you to set aside some time to reflect on your work and to identify any patterns that you see. Take time each week to read through the list of notable things you've collected and consider whether there might be something in them that's pointing you to a new idea or a new direction for your work. See if you can identify patterns and opportunities.

There have been a tremendous number of artists, entrepreneurs, and entertainers in recent years (ranging from comedian Jerry Seinfeld to hedge fund manager Ray Dalio) who have extolled the virtues of daily meditation as a way to quiet their thoughts and allow them to hear the voice of their intuition. While a description of a full meditation practice is beyond the scope of this book, I will say that the single most significant personal practice I've engaged in over the past few decades is having a period of silence for twenty minutes in the morning. During this time I try to clear my mind, listen for hunches and ideas (which I write down when they pop to mind), and quiet my nerves. Similar to the reported experiences of others, during times when I have effectively incorporated this practice into my daily routine, I've noticed an uptick in my sense of rootedness and clarity in my work.

If you are not someone who enjoys early mornings, you can structure time in the middle of your day or in between commitments to break away and listen. Regardless, taking this time for silence and reflection is critical on the road to developing your authentic voice.

HOW TO CONNECT WITH YOUR INTUITION AND IDENTITY

I was recently a keynote speaker for a conference that took place at Lake Louise in Alberta, Canada. Located in Banff National Park, the landscape is some of the most breathtaking I've experienced. After my talk, I had the rest of the day free before heading home the following morning, so I decided to go for a hike to a small tea house located about four kilometers up a mountain adjacent to the hotel. For the first leg of the trail, I passed several other hikers making their descent, but as I got higher up the mountain there were fewer passersby, and the vistas became more jaw dropping with each turn. As the trail turned back to make a pass through a patch of woods, I stopped for a moment to catch my breath and enjoy the view. I sat for a few moments, and suddenly had an unexpected sensation that something wasn't quite right. I couldn't put my finger on the problem, but there was a gnawing sense of impending trouble. I quickly ran down a mental checklist of possible problems: Was my body okay? Yes. Breathing? Yes. Was I dehydrated? Nope. Altitude issues? I don't think so. Had I subconsciously detected the presence of a grizzly bear? I wouldn't know it if I had.

Suddenly, it hit me. When it did, I was overcome with awe.

It was the silence. I couldn't hear a thing, and it was disconcerting. There was no sound of traffic or voices, not even the sound of birds. It was utter stillness, and it was something I'd not experienced in years.

After a few moments of silent attention, I noticed the faint whoosh of the wind through a mountain pass about half a kilometer away. I became aware of my own heartbeat. I was startled by the sound of my shoes as they shuffled slightly on the rocky path. I became acutely aware of everything happening around me, because there was nothing robbing my attention or clouding my senses. I spent several moments in stillness, with the sense that it's something I am meant to experience often but seem unlikely to achieve these days, in spite of my best efforts.

In the stillness, even the most minuscule observations become significant. Similarly, when we make the effort to break away from the noise of daily life, we begin to notice things that we previously overlooked. We see patterns that are blurry in our frantic activity. Even if we can't achieve the complete silence of a mountainside perch, we can still benefit from breaking away from the hustle of life and listening to our intuitive hunches, and give ourselves a chance to notice areas where we should be stepping out onto a branch. We can set aside time to listen to our inner dialogue, pay attention to how we are truly reacting to the stimuli in our environment (in ways we may not have otherwise noticed), and capture often seemingly irrelevant but potentially useful prompts that are kicking around in our minds. Silent listening is a discipline, and it requires that you carve out space in your life as a matter of practice, and embrace the potential opportunity costs associated with withdrawing from the expectations of others and the pressures of the workplace. You will not always experience breakthroughs and aha moments, but you will gain a greater sense of the context for your work, and will be better equipped to tie your daily experiences back to your through-line and consider how you might apply your voice in the course of your tasks, projects, and conversations.

Tapping into your authentic voice requires frequent breaks to "cleanse the palette" so that you have the space to intuit your inner compass. When you are in the midst of the barrage of daily influences, pressures, projects, and political calculations, this can be a challenge. You must make a practice of breaking away from the noise to listen to your hunches.

ALONE WITH YOUR THOUGHTS

So when was the last time you could say that you were actually alone with your thoughts? I don't mean sitting on a bus checking your Twitter feed, or standing in line at a coffee shop scrolling through your e-mail, or even sitting on a sofa reading a book. I mean genuinely alone with your thoughts.

I've discovered that many people—myself sometimes included—are actually afraid to think. Some of it is, in a way, a fear that deep thought yields accountability for action. (If I come up with a great idea, then I'm accountable to act on it!) It's also much more comfortable to immerse yourself in the thoughts of others, letting the milieu wash over you rather than stilling yourself and considering your life, your work, and your relationships in a thoughtful manner. Think about the following scenarios:

If you are a writer, you are paid for your ability to synthesize words with a unique perspective.

If you are an entrepreneur, your ability to see patterns, connect dots, and anticipate issues is what really sets you apart (in large part) from your competitors.

If you are a manager, your capacity for noticing the undercurrents in team dynamics is a huge part of the value you provide.

If you are a designer, it's the architecture of your concept from which everything else flows.

None of these roles can be fulfilled without intentional, sustained thought. Over time you may become skilled and experienced enough to shoot from the hip and still hit a lot of targets, but in truth you're probably compromising your best work by doing so.

HOW TO GET ALONE WITH YOUR THOUGHTS

Try it in earnest.

1. Dedicate fifteen to twenty minutes first thing in the morning, before your day ramps up.
2. Grab a notebook, a pen, and a comfortable spot.
3. Space out. You can close your eyes if you'd like, or even treat this as a form of meditation. However, unlike traditional meditation (in which the idea is extreme focus on a central thing, like your breathing or a mantra), the goal here is to actually pay attention to the flitting thoughts that cross your mind, and to follow them.
4. Write down anything that seems odd, anything that you think might require more thought, or any intuitive hunches that come to mind. This is a great time to review the previous day and see if there are any notables that come to mind.
5. If something seemingly important crosses your thoughts, follow it, build on it, and see where it goes. It's possible that you should add it to your list of notables.

You can repeat this practice a few times a day as a way of capturing your inner dialogue, or to identify what's actually going on in your brain when you're not stuffing it with stimuli from your environment.

CONNECTING THE (UNSEEN) DOTS, AND FINDING A THROUGH-LINE

Another similar method is to implement Julia Cameron's practice called Morning Pages, which was introduced in her best seller *The Artist's Way*. She suggests writing three full pages of longhand stream of consciousness first thing in the morning as a way to relieve anxiety, identify areas of stress and opportunity, and get the "gunk" out of your mind before starting in on your work. As she wrote on her blog, "Morning Pages give us a safe place to vent our hidden emotions. They urge us to be true to ourselves. They reward our honesty with forward motion. It is nearly impossible to write Morning Pages and remain stuck." This is a way of unblocking some of the intuitive thoughts that are in your head but obscured by the noise.

When I was in the early stages of working on my last book I hit an impasse. It wasn't that I didn't have a sense of what I wanted to write, it was that I had so many ideas, they flowed together with little discretion, and it was challenging to find meaningful patterns. As a result, I was prone to "shiny object syndrome," with my attention bouncing from idea to idea, and I was gaining very little meaningful traction. In the midst of my struggle, a friend suggested that I check out a book called *Accidental Genius* by Mark Levy. "It's a book about free writing," he informed me. "It will change your life." Having had many people shove books into my hands in the past using those exact terms, I was skeptical, but in my mild desperation I decided to give it a try. I started implementing Levy's techniques as a daily practice to try to gain some clarity with the book, and at first I experienced very little success. However, after about a week something changed and words were flooding out of me. Through the act of free writing, I began to cut through my mind's clutter and distill my observations into something concise and coherent. It was almost as if I had to write in order to get above the clouds of my own research and begin to see the patterns from above.

The reason that free writing can be so effective is that it allows you to bypass some of the filters and inhibitions that prevent you from gaining insight. By fluidly writing whatever thoughts come to your mind on a topic, you will make surprising discoveries about mental connections that you didn't know you possessed. You will also uncover a lot of beliefs you didn't know you had until they poured from your pen onto the page. When you are able to bypass your biases and filters, you will discover that what at first appeared to be some kind of block was actually the result of a lack of clarity of objectives, the tangling of semicontradictory expectations, or the paralysis caused by the perceived expectations of others.

One of the reasons people often ignore my advice to free write is the very reason it can be so valuable: it seems inefficient in the moment. In truth, it is. However, as in so many areas of life and work, we often confuse short-term efficiency with long-term effectiveness. This means that we fail to do the very things that will add disproportionate value in the long term while continuing to labor over short-term activities that give us a sense of forward progress, but ultimately rob us of our unique, valuable contribution.

To free write, simply take out a notebook and pen, and write whatever comes to mind during your alone time. Don't censor yourself, and don't question what you're writing. Also, don't worry about grammar and punctuation. You're not writing something to be read later (which is a big reason why people struggle to journal and free write in the first place), but simply to get things out of your head.

Once you've spent twenty to thirty minutes free writing, look back over what you've written and circle any words that seem to reoccur or patterns that emerge. Often, you'll surprise yourself with what you've written and you'll discover that you have opinions and ideas you'd never noticed, because they were drowned out by the din.

Regardless of your method, please take my encouragement to spend some time alone with your thoughts and to pay attention to what's actually happening in your mind. Notice your unique hunches and promptings. You'll be surprised at how many dots you're already connecting, if you were only listening. Use them as an opportunity to step out in unique ways and take risks with your work. The dots that connect when you are alone with your thoughts will often become critical links in your work, and will help you deepen your investment in developing and using your voice. They will point you to your through-line, and ultimately to a deeper understanding of your identity and the unique value you are capable of contributing to the world.

IMMERSE YOURSELF IN THE WORK OF YOUR HEROES

How often do you dedicate time to absorbing the work of those you admire, or learning from their tactics? Because your authentic voice is largely the product of your influences and your environment, it's essential that you continue to commune with the great minds of your field and be sharpened by them. In order to refine your perspective and your point of view, study your heroes and consider what it is you admire about their work, and how it might apply to your own.

Dedicate time to filling your well by experiencing the mentor works of your heroes or influences. Read everything you can about and by them. Learn as much as possible about their work, and consider how it applies to your own. This doesn't mean, of course, that your objective is to copy, but rather to learn and reapply whatever helps you continue to refine your own style.

CHOOSE RISK EVERY DAY

At the moment of decision, no one feels like taking a risk. Given a choice, we all tend to gravitate toward comfort rather than taking a leap into the unknown. This is why considering your work and the risks you might take ahead of time can be helpful in creating accountability to act, and also in relieving the pressure to risk it all at once.

As you consider your upcoming work, think about one or two strategic risks that you plan to take in order to differentiate yourself from others around you. Where has your work grown a bit stale? Where are you playing it too safe? Where are you afraid to let your work lead you, but know that you need to go anyway?

As you look back on your life and the ultimate shaping of your authentic voice, you will find that it was the small risks that eventually led to big results. Where is your intuition telling you to place small bets?

COMPARE YOUR ACTIONS AND YOUR TENETS

As you survey your upcoming work, your meetings, and your conversations, how can you infuse more of your choices with a sense of personal mission and identity? Are you clear about how your choices speak to what you care about?

It's never cut-and-dried, which is what makes it so challenging. However, it's in the small choices that a big voice is forged. Staying true to yourself is easy when no one is watching, but when all eyes are upon you it can feel like there is more to lose. Getting ahead of the game by looking at your upcoming choices and considering them through the lens of personal passion will help you be less reactionary.

1. Take a few minutes to review the tenets that you've established for your work through your manifesto.
2. Consider the decisions you've made with your work over the past week or two, and whether they are reflective of who you are and what you care about.
3. Consider your upcoming work, and how you can better align your decisions and actions with your core tenets in order to find expression for your authentic voice.

VISION: KNOWING YOUR AUDIENCE

One persistent challenge of work is that we must keep one foot rooted in the present (today's tasks and projects) while moving forward with a vision for where the work might be leading us. It's this tension that often derails us. We have to hold both of these realities in our mind at the same time in our effort to close the gap.

As you strive to craft your work with precision and shape it according to your vision, you must remember that it's the microalignments that matter most. Staying true to yourself and to your audience is a daily battle.

ARE YOU VEERING OFF COURSE, OR DIVERGING?

As an audit, take a few minutes today to consider the choices you've made with your work over the past week, month, or quarter. Are there any choices you've made that seem inconsistent with where you want your work to be headed? Are there any choices that seem out of character for you? Where does your work lack precision, consonance, and consistency?

If there is something that seems a little off course, is it because you are choosing to diverge and explore new territory, or is it due to a lack of diligence with regard to your vision? The former is perfectly fine, as long as it's intentional. However, the latter can lead to a growing gap between your desired work and your actual work.

In those areas where you see that you are veering unintentionally, what are some different choices you can make with your work to bring it back on course?

DEFINING YOUR INTENDED AUDIENCE

As you look at your current list of projects, do you have a clear understanding of your intended audience for each? Do you know precisely who you are creating for? If not, this is step one. Take a look at your projects through the lens of your IA. Try to be as precise as possible, and whenever you can, consider a specific person.

If you're stuck, imagine that you're having a conversation with your IA about the project. Share your idea with them, and imagine their response. Is there anything that's confusing to them or needs further refinement? Is there anything that you thought would be appropriate but is actually irrelevant? It may seem silly to engage in an imaginary conversation, but you might be surprised at the kinds of serendipitous insights that arise through this kind of mental play.

CRAFT THE PRESS RELEASE FIRST

Here's how project work tends to flow: an idea is chosen and crafted into a product or solution, and afterward you start trying to figure out how to make it appealing to your intended audience. However, a better solution is often to work backward from the audience to the product. One strategy that I've found effective is to begin by writing a one-page press release. This tactic, championed by Amazon founder Jeff Bezos, is used at the beginning of any large project in order to help his teams stay focused and avoid "project drift." All of their projects begin with an internal press release announcing the finished product, and if the feature set doesn't sound appealing enough, then it is either scrapped or refined until it's ready for the next step.

This tactic can also be helpful in pushing through blocks and challenges in your work. Often, the reason we get stuck is because we have lost sight of what we're really trying to do or who we're really trying to reach. By stopping midterm to write a press release, you reground yourself in the central idea of the project, which will likely also help you regain your footing.

STEEP YOURSELF IN EMPATHY

Another way to stay deeply connected and to refine your vision for your work is to regularly empathize with the problems your intended audience is facing. To do this, you can engage in the four-step empathy process: decide, identify, recall, act.

Decide: Choose to engage with your audience in an empathetic manner. Remind yourself of why your work is important, and how you plan to impact the lives of others through your efforts. Then consider a problem that your IA is facing.

Identify: Connect the problem you were facing with the problem your IA is facing. How are they similar? In what ways can you identify with your IA?

Recall: Remember a time when you faced a similar problem in your life and work. How did you feel? How did the problem affect you?

Act: Consider what would have helped you when you were in a similar situation to your IA's. What could someone have done to serve you? How could they have made your life better, or equipped you to improve your situation?

This practice will take time, and may not always yield groundbreaking results in the short term, but over time you will find that you are more connected with your audience and are better able to create more resonant and impactful work. If you are a part of a team, I'd also encourage you to have this conversation regularly. It will reveal areas where team members differ in their understanding of the needs of your audience, and provide a chance to sharpen your vision.

MASTERY: SHARPEN YOUR SKILLS

Of the three drivers of voice, none gives you freedom of expression like mastery of your skills and platform. No matter how invested and unique your work, or how refined your vision, without the right skills you will not be able to bring it to life. Additionally, if you lack a sense of context and timing, your work might be met with a resounding silence from your audience.

STAY IMMERSED IN RELEVANT STIMULI

Just like paying attention to mentor works can help you refine your sense of uniqueness and mission, immersing yourself in relevant stimuli can help you begin to identify patterns in your field. While you don't want to become overwhelmed or awash in too much detail or get distracted, paying attention to the leading thoughts and trends of your industry can allow you to stay ahead of potential opportunities to put your voice into the mix.

Dedicate time on your calendar each week to absorbing stimuli relevant to your work and vision, or that inspires you to think about your work in a new way. Consider how it impacts your perception of your work and your audience, including any new ideas or avenues to pursue. Inspiration will often strike in the least likely of places, and often outside the places you would normally look, so always absorb stimuli through the lens of your identity and vision.

DEDICATE "DEEP WORK TIME" TO INVEST IN YOURSELF

Brilliant work is expensive. Anything of value that you wish to create will require a significant investment of time.

I recently came across a new phrase while reading the book *Essentialism* by Greg McKeown—"monk mode." McKeown was reflecting upon how the process of writing a book was taking a toll on him, especially in light of his existing commitments to business, family, and friends. He determined that he was going to go into monk mode for the following several months, declining all new invitations and opportunities, until his book was completed. He dedicated five A.M. to one P.M. every day for nine months to the process of writing his book.

While appealing in concept, most people who hear this story would say, "That's great if you can manage it, but I don't have that kind of discretion over my time." I agree that most roles don't allow this kind of latitude, but I'd challenge you to consider how the core principle might be applied nonetheless. You don't need to dedicate eight hours a day to one project or to developing one skill, but you can still carve out dedicated time for your most important work while closing the door to distractions and interruptions. Start with an hour or two a few times per week, and set it on your calendar.

Professor and author Cal Newport calls this process "deep work." He argues that the most effective way to produce high-quality output on a project is to routinely dedicate chunks of time to accomplishing it. This is contrary to how most people I encounter in the marketplace actually think about their work. Instead, they attempt to do their creative work in the cracks of their already busy meeting schedule, or in between the more urgent e-mails beckoning them from their tyrannical in-box.

I've experienced the same effects through long periods of uninterrupted, focused time in my work, and have discovered that my sense of the work, my timing, and my overall mastery of the process is much improved when I give myself the appropriate amount of space to think deeply and shape the work. I've found that assigning time blocks to specific projects or tasks is often more effective than putting them on task lists, because it gives me permission to focus on one thing at a time. Brilliant work is expensive because there is often a lot of "churn." It may take two hours to do thirty minutes of solid, productive, contributive work.

You must be willing to invest large chunks of time in yourself and your work. Efficiency is great, when you can achieve it, but you cannot sacrifice long-term effectiveness on the altar of short-term efficiency.

1. Choose a particular project that's important to you, or a skill that you want to develop, and dedicate three blocks of time (at least an hour each) this week to working on it.
2. During that time, turn off all notifications, and if possible remove yourself from potential distractions.

3. If something comes up that could interfere with your plans, then politely decline and say that you already have a commitment during that time.

If your work is important to you, then it deserves dedicated time on your calendar. It's an investment in yourself, in your body of work, and, ultimately, in shaping your authentic voice.

CREATE AN ENVIRONMENT FOR EASY EXPERIMENTATION

Our oldest son has been showing an interest in the guitar for a few years. When he first indicated he might want to learn to play, we bought him a reasonably priced guitar that I knew would serve his purposes. However, the guitar mostly sat in the closet in its case for several months. One day, I had a flash of insight about how I might help him. I realized that whenever he wanted to practice guitar, he had to go to his closet, remove the guitar from its (tight, ill-fitting) case, ensure it was in tune, then carry it across the room to his bed in order to play it. I thought that perhaps "out of sight, out of mind," combined with the extra steps necessary to play, might be preventing him from casual practice. I went to the basement and dug through old bins until I found a wall-mount guitar stand I'd used in my home office prior to our recent move. I went to his room, mounted the stand, and hung his guitar prominently on the wall beside his bed. Now it would be the first thing he saw when he entered his room.

These days, my wife and I routinely have to ask him to stop playing late at night so that his brother and sister can get some sleep. Often his first instinct when entering the room is to pick up the guitar and strum for a few minutes. Just through that one simple act of removing barriers to practice, he has improved markedly. It created an environment of easy experimentation, because the tools were present and readily available whenever he wanted them.

How can you create an environment of easy experimentation in your work? What tools or resources can you prominently place in your environment to encourage playing with ideas, developing your skills, or forging new forms of expression in your work?

FORM YOUR COLLECTIVE

Finally, know that your relationships will impact your work as much as any other factor in your life. Whom do you turn to for unvarnished truth? Who sharpens your skills and challenges you to be better than you were yesterday? Who calls your bluff when you're coasting or playing it too safe?

In *The Accidental Creative* I called groups of five to seven people who get together frequently to discuss work Circles, and offered three questions you can ask to help one another:

> What are you working on right now?
>
> What resources can we bring to the table to help you in your work?
>
> What's inspiring you right now?

These three questions provide a powerful framework for conversation about life and work and will help you stay on track.

Mastery of your work is about daily, committed, focused progress on the skills and intuition that allow you to bring your ideas to life. The greater your mastery, the more latitude you will have and the more opportunities you will be able to take advantage of. Define the skills that you need to develop, then dedicate focus, time, and energy each week to doing so. Over time, as you build momentum, your understanding of your voice will grow along with it.

While much of this book has focused on your individual voice and how to develop it in the course of your work, many of us must work in collaboration with others. This adds a lot of complexity to the mix, because it raises questions about how to merge the different perspectives and ideas of the group into one cohesive voice. However, as you'll find, that very real challenge can often become a team's greatest opportunity to shine.

Chapter 8

Developing Your Team's Voice

One word expresses the pathway to greatness: voice.
Those on this path find their voice and inspire others to
find theirs. The rest never do.

—Stephen R. Covey

You've probably heard it said that leading a group of talented, creative people is like herding cats. They will go where they want to go, and the challenge is to keep them focused and corral them in the proper direction. However, I think that this is a very short-sighted analogy, and the damage it does to team dynamics likely outweighs any consolation it provides for frustrated leaders. In truth, most people I encounter want to do great work, and are anything but self-centered and obsessed with their own agenda. Rather, I've found that most people deeply desire to be something bigger than themselves. However, in order for a leader to help them connect to that deeper mission, they must have a compelling vision and the ability to help them channel their talents in a meaningful way.

While the advice in this chapter is broadly applicable to anyone functioning in a team environment, it is largely targeted at those who have influence over the strategic actions and daily activity of the team. However, in a marketplace where collectives and loose teams of collaborators are increasingly becoming the norm, everyone needs to understand how their individual voice affects the overall voice and effectiveness of any group of which they are a part.

THE LEADER AS DOT CONNECTOR

As a child, I used to love connect-the-dots books, and the more complex they were, the better. I would spend hours searching for the next numbered dot, drawing the lines, and trying to guess what the underlying picture might be. Inevitably, even before the dots were completely connected, a pattern would suddenly emerge and the picture I was drawing would be quite obvious. It wasn't there, and then it was. One line made the difference.

Not to be too reductive, but creative work feels very similar to a giant game of connect the dots. You are searching for the next clue, the next hunch to follow, the next idea, and then suddenly a pattern snaps into place and the right path seems obvious. It wasn't, and then suddenly it is. There is a lot of work left to do to finish the project, but an image is now fixed in your mind of how it's all going to develop.

The role of the leader in this process is to place the dots. Your job is to ensure that the team is exploring the right set of options, and looking in the right places for the ideas. You are not telling them what to think or how to do it, but you are ensuring that they are operating with the proper understanding of identity and role, functioning within the proper vision, and utilizing the appropriate skills in order to get to where the team is trying to go. You have to stay only one dot ahead of your team, but you have to be very clear about your expectations.

THE COMPLEXITIES OF THE COLLECTIVE VOICE

There are many additional factors that make finding your voice as a team challenging. Although a diversity of viewpoints and skills often makes for a stronger unit, that very same dynamic can make the process of doing the work infinitely more challenging. Learning to work with one another's strengths and quirks takes precious time and energy, and this is why many teams simply settle into bad patterns over time and never truly find their collective voice.

Personal preference must be subverted. When working as a team, it's often the case that your personal opinions and hunches will not be shared by the majority of those around you. No matter how much you try to argue your case, you simply cannot seem to sway others to your opinion. This can undoubtedly be frustrating, especially if you've spent a lot of time refining your ideas and you are convinced that you are correct. However, the moment you join a team, you make a subtle pact that your individual will is now subservient to the collective will of your teammates. Does that make them correct in every instance? Of course not. Is it fair? No. It's simply the nature of teamwork.

Many people stall their careers because they can't develop the ability to work on someone else's idea as if it were their own. The beauty of developing an authentic voice is that you are able to contribute value to a project even when you fundamentally disagree with the direction it's taking. However, you recognize that the ultimate outcome matters more than whether you get to have your way.

Teams tend to become homogenous over time. No matter how talented they are, and regardless of their initial vector, it's inevitable that teams tend to gravitate over time toward the easiest path. I was once invited to speak at an event in Denver, and at lunch following the event a creative director for a local agency shared a great analogy for how he's seen teams settle into stasis. He asked me to imagine four people holding up a bed sheet, with each person holding a corner. Then he asked me to imagine a marble is dropped somewhere on the sheet. "What will happen to the marble?" he asked me. The answer is that the four people are likely to work together—subconsciously, perhaps—to stabilize the marble. The only way to do that is to keep it in the middle.

"That's exactly what happens on teams," he told me. "Because we tend to prize stability, we eventually do whatever it takes to preserve it, even if it means gravitating to the middle and doing underwhelming work."

I found this to be an astute description of how mediocrity creeps into a team over time. It begins with small compromises, and individuals refusing to use their voices, and it culminates in an everyday "go with the flow" attitude. To countermand this requires a deep commitment to allowing divergent opinions and an equally deep willingness to cultivate dissent and discontent within the team. While on the surface this may seem to be a recipe for strife and frustration, it's actually the key to allowing your team to shape its collective voice over time.

You are both pulled (by market) and pushed (by mission). There is an intricate balance to be struck between meeting the expressed needs of your audience and pursuing the inner goals of your organization. When you become too fixated on serving your customers what they want, there is always a chance that you will miss opportunities to innovate and exceed their expectations. At the same time, when you become too internally focused on your own priorities, you might create something that lacks empathy or misses the mark entirely. As such, finding a collective team voice is a tightrope walk of understanding what your audience desires while also fueling your work with a sense of purpose and mission that is independent from market forces. The most effective teams are able to take the perceptions and desires of their consumers into account while also being willing to push them beyond their present comfort zone.

REACTIVE LEADERSHIP LEADS TO WITHDRAWAL

When the vision lacks clarity, or there is little trust within a team, it's often because a leader is operating reactively rather than setting a clear tone and direction for the work. When this happens, it makes it difficult for team members to engage fully in the process, because they are unsure if they are headed in the right direction. Team members may even begin to withdraw from the process until a clear decision is made about a project, which is a perfectly logical, self-protective response. It's frustrating to pour yourself into something that you know is likely to change in a week. The net result is that a team lacks the full involvement of its members, and thus its collective voice is squelched.

The only way to avoid this is to ensure that there is a clear vision for the work, and that whoever is responsible for setting the direction for a project is making effective and clear decisions. This will allow everyone to engage fully and add their individual voice to the mix.

To overcome these (and other) forces that lead to lackluster, down-the-middle work requires diligence. It takes a focused effort on the part of the leader to ground the team in a sense of identity, to cull a sharp and defining vision, and to establish expectations around growth and skill development.

IDENTITY: ESTABLISHING THE BATTLE LINES

For individuals, how we choose to spend our focus, assets, time, and energy ultimately determines the quality of our end result. If we spend these scarce resources in the pursuit of clear, valuable goals, then we are likely to make meaningful progress. If instead we spend them frivolously, then we are likely to end up far from our charted course. It seems easy and obvious to think about this on an individual level, but when you multiply this principle times the number of people on a team, the effects of well-placed or misplaced effort are massive. A slight misalignment can mean missing the mark in a big way.

Thus, it's important that a leader constantly refines the team's sense of identity and mission, and helps individuals understand how their voice plays into the overall direction of the team. The best team members elevate one another by bringing their best rather than attempting to wrestle the team into following their own agenda. Seth Goldman, cofounder of Honest Tea, described the challenge of keeping a talented team on the same page. With regard to steering a team toward a common mission, Goldman told me that the most important thing is instilling a sense of ownership throughout the organization. "I tell my senior management team, 'I want you talking not just from your perspective, I want you talking as a business owner. The worst thing I see is when we're having a meeting and the marketing part is done, and the production part begins, and the marketing person pulls out her BlackBerry. I'll stop and say, 'What, you're no longer a part of the company?'" The team needs to be vested in every decision, as if they owned the business themselves. When traveling, it's not uncommon for Honest Tea executives to share hotel rooms or to eat on the cheap because they want to spend those dollars investing in the growth of the business, not throwing them away on unnecessary travel expenses.

"It's really important to make sure you understand every part of the business, and if you don't you'll become typecast and won't be consulted on important decisions."

Instilling this sense of ownership means helping everyone understand the core, mission-driven nature of the team and showing them how to own the tenets that make the team unique.

UNDERSTANDING THE MISSION

The through-line, or core reason for being, must be apparent to all team members, and it's important that the leader loops back to it continuously. If you want the team to work with a consistent and compelling voice, then this context is important, especially when the work is complex and there are a lot of opportunities for team members to drift off course. Just like a personal set of tenets, or a manifesto, can be helpful in rooting your personal work in the principles that matter deeply, teams benefit greatly from a core set of grounding principles that keep them focused on the main objective.

The sense of collective identity your team holds is rooted largely in the narrative that it lives by, and this means understanding the greater aim of the work and the mission the team is on. While many organizations have lofty mission statements (that often seem largely irrelevant to daily operations), it can help to have a team manifesto (using the process prescribed for individuals in chapter 4), which will provide a quick and dirty set of principles that define team culture and help each person understand how their work is funneling up into a greater purpose. These principles can be established by answering— as a team—a set of questions, such as:

What problem(s) are we uniquely qualified to solve?

Who/what is our common "enemy"?

What great opportunity are we chasing?

What fills us with compassionate anger?

What makes us special / called out?

While it's a little naïve to think that everyone will want to view their work as part of a grand mission or adventure, it is important that each person sees how their individual work connects to the answers to the above questions. If nothing else, the answers provide a framework for helping team members make critical decisions about where they are allocating their focus, assets, time, and energy.

One method that can help teams stay aligned and speak with one voice is a quick weekly check-in to help each team member understand how their work ties into the overall through-line of the team. A simple five-minute meeting with each team member can help a leader reinforce the overall identity/mission of the team and relate each member's individual work back to that mission. Additionally, a quick check-in can help the leader stay attuned to how each team member is feeling about the work they are doing. A few questions that can help during check-ins include:

Do you understand why your work is important to team objectives?

What are you most excited about this week, and why?

Is there anything I can do to clear a path for you?

Although these sound like simple questions, it's amazing how easy it is to overlook the obvious as we're dealing with the uncertainty of daily work and decision making.

DEFINING THE CULTURE

An additional method for helping the team stay aligned around a common sense of identity is to codify the most uniquely defining elements of your culture. This means developing a set of tenets, or a framework for what matters most to the team, and listing the kinds of behaviors that will be rewarded and commended. One team that I worked with created a thirty-one-day desk calendar, with each day containing a critical element of the team's culture and why it was important. Another team posted their clearly defined tenets in a public place, and would start each weekly meeting by talking about one of them and whether the team had been living up to it.

There's another benefit to developing a strong set of well-defined and public tenets for your team: hiring. It's a great way to gauge whether or not a potential hire is the right fit for the team. Just because someone has the right skills does not mean that they will be a cultural match, so the earlier you have the conversation about culture and identity, the more likely you are to find team members who naturally mesh with your team narrative.

VISION: SHAPING THE ARC OF THE WORK

If your team's sense of identity is about who you are and what you stand for, its vision is about where you are going and who you will impact through your work. It's about connecting with your core intended audience and ensuring that everyone's daily work is shaped by their understanding of how it will ultimately impact the people you serve.

Most teams have a general sense of who their audience or customer is, but over time it's easy for this understanding to become dulled or confused. As such, it becomes much more difficult for team members to retain a clear vision for their work, or to make bold decisions in the interest of their audience.

Remember that the best, most impactful work results not just from what you care about (Identity), but also what your audience cares about (Vision), and an ability to connect with them through a set of relevant skills (Mastery). It's at the intersection of these three elements of the Voice Engine that your team's most resonant work will be accomplished.

HOME BASE: DEFINING THE INTENDED AUDIENCE

Does your team have a clear understanding of your intended audience and how you hope to impact them? This is the single most important thing to hold in mind as they work, as it is the factor that allows them to make critical decisions and take strategic risks.

As mentioned in the earlier chapter on vision, it's tempting to generalize your intended audience by targeting a group or psychographic, but this can have limited benefit. It's almost always more effective to conjure a specific person or small group of people when you are creating. You want to hold those people in mind as you have conversations about products, strategy, and communication.

If you've not had the intended audience conversation with your team in a while, it's something you should consider. In fact, it's probably a good idea to revisit it at least three or four times a year to ensure that (a) you are all still in agreement on the specifics of your IA, (b) any newcomers to the team can be brought up to speed on how their work is important to the overall mission of the organization, and (c) any work in progress can be measured against the target.

Here are a few questions to help you clarify whether your team is aligned in its understanding of intended audience:

Who are we really trying to serve with our work? (Not theoretically, but practically. Give specific examples of how your team's work will improve their lives.)

Who are we currently serving with our work, and is it the right person?

Is there anything we are doing right now that is inconsistent with the desires of the intended audience we are trying to reach?

What one thing could we do to better connect with our intended audience?

Asking these questions several times a year will help your team members keep the intended audience top of mind as they go about their day. It's not a foolproof method, but it does create a kind of accountability and helps prevent mission-creep, in which you unintentionally shift your focus in small ways that over time add up to a major misalignment.

IN THE WEEDS: CULTIVATING EMPATHY FOR YOUR INTENDED AUDIENCE
It's highly possible to define your intended audience, but not really know or understand them. In order to make your team's authentic

voice resonate, you must create work that touches your intended audience in a place of need or aspiration. This might mean solving a problem, offering an outlet, or providing education or encouragement, but in the end you are improving the life of your intended audience in some way. It's easy to lose touch with this when you are in the weeds of your work, and when your immediate line of focus is on checking off tasks and pushing through projects. However, keeping the core "why" in front of you as you work will help you make better decisions.

The four-step process described by SEEK can be of benefit in conversation with your team: decide, identify, recall, act.

Decide: Before you dive into a task or project, or before you make a major decision as a team, decide that you are going to function with empathy for your intended audience. While it might be tempting to skip this step, it can be valuable to mark the moment at the beginning of your work and remind yourself of why it's important at all.

Identify: Consider a time, as a team, when you experienced the same problem that your intended audience is experiencing. What were the circumstances, and how was the event significant to you at the time?

Recall: Think about how that circumstance affected you. How did you feel? What did it do to impede your effectiveness in other areas of your life or work? How did it affect your relationships or your ability to function?

Act: Based upon your answers to the previous questions, consider how you might act now and how you should shape your work so that it lines up with the needs of your intended audience. Infuse your work with an empathetic understanding of their needs rather than simply functioning reactively or in a self-centered manner.

Again, this small pause at the beginning of a project requires precious time and energy, and can seem like a nonessential step or something to check off a list. However, by infusing your work with a sense of empathy and connectedness to your intended audience, you will increase the chances that your team will work with one voice and reach its desired impact.

You are not working for the sake of it. You are hopefully trying to have real impact in the world, which means changing the lives of the people you exist to serve. By rooting yourself in a common vision, and reinforcing that vision on a regular basis, you will increase the odds that your team will stay aligned and effective.

MASTERY: OWNING YOUR SPACE AND YOUR PROCESS

Once your team has rooted its efforts in both a strong sense of identity and a clear and compelling vision for how its work will impact the intended audience, it's time to ensure that your timing and skill set are aligned with where you want the work to go.

The core mission of the Always team and their empathetic vision for their intended audience had always been present, but it was only when those two factors were combined with a well-timed campaign (#LikeA Girl), one that connected with emerging cultural themes, that they saw massive impact.

Of course, this doesn't mean chasing trends or trying to fabricate something inauthentic in order to take advantage of a cultural phenomenon, but it does mean paying attention to the broader marketplace and ensuring that you are having conversations about how these themes might affect your own work. The answer may be "Very little to not at all," but the conversation ensures that you aren't missing opportunities to introduce your team's voice into the mix of what's happening in the marketplace and the broader culture.

CALLING YOUR SHOTS: GETTING THE TIMING RIGHT

Most innovations are the result of a long period of intuitive action and small risk that culminates in an apparent and sudden-seeming breakthrough. In truth, that breakthrough is rarely as sudden as it appears from the outside because there have been layers upon layers of effort, risk, and trial and error involved in the "overnight success." Author Steven Johnson calls this the "slow hunch," meaning that it was the persistent pursuit of an idea over a long period of time that resulted in the aha moment. Without that persistent effort, valuable innovation would have been unlikely.

In the same way, any single conversation about patterns and trends is unlikely to yield tremendous value, but the layering of those conversations over time will help your team plot its place in the wider landscape of the marketplace and ensure that you are taking the appropriate small risks that will help you move collectively in the right direction.

Once again, a simple and regular conversation with your team can bring these patterns into the light. Additionally, by including all team members in a conversation about what they are seeing and potential opportunities for action you are opening the aperture and letting more ideas into the mix, which can help you spot patterns more effectively.

Here are a few questions that can be of value in this team conversation:

What opportunity do you think we are missing right now? Where should we intentionally be looking?

What overall trends or patterns are you noticing with our intended audience? Have there been any surprising conversations?

What excites you most right now about the next six months?

What worries you most about the next six months?

What is inspiring you or filling your well right now? How do you see it applying to your work?

If you could start doing any one thing right now, what would it be?

You may be surprised at the answers that come back to you from your team. It is likely that you will find that they see things that you don't, and that what excites them is far afield from where you are presently focused. This conversation also provides the team with a chance to express things for which there is no other forum, or which seem irrelevant to their daily work. The best opportunities are often missed because we are so focused on what must be done at the expense of what might be done.

GAME OF INCHES: MASTERING THE DAILIES

Just like having a set of daily practices can help individuals develop their voice and gain greater context for their place in the world, teams can root themselves in a set of daily practices to help them better communicate and stay focused. Leaders can encourage team members to immerse themselves daily in stimuli that are likely to spark ideas, or to engage in meaningful conversations with peers that help them understand the overall mind-set of the team.

For team leaders and members, there are five core areas that can act as containers for these practices. (I covered these in *The Accidental Creative* as the elements of Creative Rhythm, and go into greater detail there.) Below are some questions that can be asked daily to help you develop the team's voice:

Focus: Ensure that your finite attention is focused in the right place, and against the right problems.

Do I/we understand the main problem we're trying to solve with this project? Has the problem been clearly defined as it relates to our intended audience?

What are our top priorities today/this week, and are they clear to everyone on the team?

Relationships: Structure your team such that there are meaningful conversations happening about how the work is getting done, not just what is getting done.

Are there any open relational loops that need to be closed?

Is there any open conflict on the team, or misunderstanding that needs to be resolved?

Is there anyone who needs to be encouraged or shown why their work is important to the team's efforts?

Energy: This is about ensuring that you are not squeezing all of the available "white space" out of the team's day, but are leaving room to think and innovate.

What project(s) need to be pruned so that we have space?

What should I/we say no to today in order to free us up?

What decisions do I need to make so that other team members are not waiting on me?

Stimuli: Fill your well with high-quality stimuli so that you are stoking the fires of your creativity and fueling your voice.

What inspiring resource will I/we read/experience and share with others today?

What have I/we learned or noticed lately that I need to share with someone today?

What open question do I/we have that I will pursue an answer to today, whether through a resource or through another person?

Hours: Ensure that you are spending your time effectively, not just efficiently.

What time will I/we dedicate today to thinking deeply about a problem our team is facing?

What strategic, calculated risk will I/we take today with the work?

Not all of these questions must be asked daily, of course, but they provide a framework for the sorts of questions that you will find valuable in assessing how you should structure your day. The worst thing you can do is to allow yourself to be carried along by your work, and to thus lose sight of the team's core productive passion and voice. Implementing a daily set of questions and practices ensures that you won't drift too far from your core.

FINAL THOUGHTS FOR LEADERS

The leader plays a key role in unlocking the voice of a team. The leader must set the right boundaries for the team, while also directing strategic exploration and risk taking in areas most likely to lead to breakthroughs.

Here are the five principles that I believe every leader of creative teams must live by if they want to help their team find its collective voice.

1. BE A LASER, NOT A LIGHTHOUSE.

Many leaders are so concerned about safety that they spend much of their time talking about what not to do versus what to do. They operate more like a lighthouse than a laser. A lighthouse can tell you only where not to go, but can't provide any kind of precise direction or alternative. Creative teams need precise, focused direction. Instead, a leader needs to make key decisions that nudge their team in the right direction. Your team needs you to tell them what to do, not what not to do.

2. ENCOURAGE DISSENT, FOSTER DISCONTENT.

Healthy teams have a level of dissent in their strategic conversations. You know your team is in trouble when there is no disagreement. It means one of the following is probably happening:

> People are too comfortable to risk speaking up. No one wants to rock the boat.

> No one is really thinking. There is a lack of true ownership of vision. People are doing their jobs and nothing more.

> There's a general lack of accountability for the work, or accountability is spread too thin to matter.

You encourage dissent on a team by rewarding strong, focused opinions. If you want something to happen, reward it. Encourage people when they share a contrary opinion. Change your mind and admit that you were wrong, publicly. Foster strong conversations about direction and fuel the passion of your team members.

At the same time, you must foster discontent with the current level of the work. You do this by reframing the conversation. Instead of comparing your work with other, similar work by other companies or teams, reframe expectations by expanding the team's view of what's possible. Instead of being the best brand design firm on the block, reframe the goal as being the best at creating customer experiences or capturing marketplace attention. Instead of being the best copywriter, reframe the goal as being the best at framing marketplace narrative. Always be pushing your team to new heights. Don't allow them to settle.

3. DEFEND YOUR TEAM TO THE DEATH.

Do you know the fastest path to permanent failure as a creative leader? Sell out your team, just once. Nothing else will ever matter. Once you've lost their trust, you will never regain it.

Here's a principle worth tattooing on your hand: the leader gets to take the most arrows. If you're going to lead a team, you are responsible and accountable for the final work, including the creative choices made and the execution thereof. Everyone wants to be the leader, but few really want to lead. Your team must see you defending them when it counts most. If they do, then they will be there to defend you when you make a risky choice that fails or when you overextend on your interpersonal bank account. They have to know that you are right there beside them, also taking daily strategic risks in the pursuit of great work.

If you want to find your team's voice, the leader has to go first. Defend your team to the death.

4. THINK BACKWARD/FORWARD.

Closely related to principle number 3, you must remember that you are not the only one expending effort to make things happen. People on your team have poured their blood, sweat, and tears into their work. They die many deaths in the pursuit of brilliance. But as leaders, the only thing that often matters is "What have you done for me lately?"

Do not cheapen the sacrifice of your team by forgetting their past triumphs. Many of your team members have spent themselves to the point of exhaustion in order make the team successful. Don't forget that in a moment of weakness, whether yours or theirs.

5. BE CLEAR, EVEN WHEN UNCERTAIN.

Here's a dirty little secret: you don't have to have all the answers. (In fact, if you think you do, you're probably not as good of a leader as you think you are.) But even when you don't know the answer, you must be clear about your expectations. When you aren't, your team is likely to spin out into misery. You must be clear about your expectations even when you're not certain of the way forward.

Vision diffuses, meaning that it disperses through the air and gets less precise as the project proceeds. You must, therefore, begin with incredible precision. Then you must communicate your objectives clearly, even when you don't have all the answers. Many leaders leave room for ambiguity because they're insecure about their own abilities. This lack of clarity trickles down and makes things unnecessarily complex, which leads to a lack of motivation within the ranks.

If you want your team to do its best work, you must be clear, even when you are uncertain that you have made the right decision.

Ralph Nader once stated, "I start with the premise that the function of leadership is to produce more leaders, not more followers." Your objective as the leader of a team should be to help the team develop and implement its own unique, authentic voice, while keeping one eye on the overall mission of the organization. This can be a tricky balancing act, but all great work is born from this tension. In fact, the elimination of tension is the elimination of the possibility of greatness. Free your team, provide solid guidelines and clear expectations, and stoke the fire of their curiosity through regular conversation, and you will help them channel their individual passion into your team's collective voice.

Chapter 9

Up the Curve

An ounce of action is worth a ton of theory.

—Friedrich Engels

In the hundreds of interviews I've conducted with brilliant contributors, two words come up over and over when I ask them about how they developed such a unique style: action and patience. In the mad dash to gain recognition and success, it's easy to latch on to early victories and squeeze them for all they're worth, but those who embrace a disciplined, long-arc pursuit of brilliance are the ones who work their way onto a path of unique and valuable contribution. To win in the long term, you sometimes have to be willing to go back to the beginning in order to keep moving forward. You also have to let your work be messy while you figure out where it's all leading you.

In discussing the tendency to perfect things too soon in the process, Donald Knuth, the acclaimed computer scientist and professor, argued in a paper that "premature optimization is the root of all evil."

Energy should not be wasted trying to optimize code until the true bottlenecks, central purpose, and structure of the program are refined. Kevin Kelly, cofounder of *WIRED* magazine, picked up on Knuth's phrase and applied it to life and work. In an interview for the Tim Ferriss podcast, he said that many people want to turn a momentary success into something more permanent by immediately attempting to optimize it and maximize its value. The problem, Kelly argues, is that we often don't know precisely what we want at the early stages of life, or even in the early stages of a long project. Thus, premature optimization can actually inhibit the kind of wandering that is necessary in order to uncover loose, disparate connections and synthesize meaning out of seemingly unrelated ideas. This can be especially true for those who achieve a measure of early success, Kelly argued. Once there is something to protect, it's often easier to become overly cautious and assume a more defensive posture in work rather than an offensive one.

An unfortunate side effect of premature optimization is becoming a caricature of one's self, and thus losing precision and poignancy. In the attempt to replicate and optimize early success, it's easy to focus on the external contributors to short-term success, such as a favorable personality, raw skill, or even work ethic, at the expense of the core drivers of long-term effectiveness, such as the ability to spot and take advantage of opportunities, and a core vision for your work. Thus, many people try to replicate early success by going back to the same tactics, and after a while they become stale and predictable. We've seen this with everything from products to TV sitcoms. Once the formula becomes too predictable, it grows stale. It's obvious to everyone when love for the work has dissipated and all that's left is a desire for the external recognition that accompanies it.

Sometimes breaking away from your routine—or even stepping away from it for a season—can open new ways of seeing your work and help you avoid this kind of premature optimization. riCardo Crespo spent the early years of his career as a designer and creative director at large ad agencies before making the leap to running the creative teams at Mattel and 20th Century Fox. While his unique, diverse career allowed him to rub elbows with brilliant artists, creators, filmmakers, and business leaders, a few years ago he began to realize that his career was no longer scratching a deep itch he'd had since his early days as a young designer. "I came to realize that—while I was confident living in the boardroom environment and adding a lot of value inside a large organization—the question I'd been ignoring for several years was do I want to?" He'd grown a bit tired of what he considered to be "the game," and said that he initially shrugged off those instincts, but over time they began to obsess his thoughts. "One thing I've learned over time," he told me, "is that you can't lie to the person in the mirror." He began considering what life outside a traditional organizational role might look like, and after a season of discussion with his wife and family, he informed the company that he would be leaving indefinitely on sabbatical. "It was really about finding my 'why.' I realized that for so long I'd been somewhat trained to comply, and that I'd lost my own voice a bit in the effort to stick with the company script. I needed to get back in touch with what made me someone who could intelligently provoke and provide fresh, outside perspective."

He immediately began receiving calls from headhunters and corporate recruiters trying to lure him with promises of money and prestigious roles inside some amazing companies. "It was really hard to say no," he told me. "Especially since a few of these companies were the kind that people would give up anything to work for." He politely declined all offers, which only made them want him more. They continued to court him with more money, better opportunity, and more visibility. Again, he declined all offers. "However, I told them that I would be willing to take on work on a project-by-project basis. Not as an employee of the company, and not as a consultant, but as an adviser." A few companies jumped on his offer, and soon his "sabbatical" was full of those same boardroom and C-suite conversations as before, only this time it felt different. "It was a subtle shift, but now I was working with them, not for them. I was able to try out my voice in a lot of different contexts, and communicate from the role of adviser rather than as an employee. It allowed me to approach my work as a consumer first, then a marketer, instead of the other way around."

Crespo says that his ongoing sabbatical experiment may not be permanent, but it has allowed him a renewed ability to be himself, and to challenge others in a relatively low-risk way. It's what these companies are paying him to do—speak truth in an authentic way. "Being authentic means never having to say you're sorry," Crespo says. "If you are authentic in all of the ways that matter, it means that you will never have to backtrack and apologize for what you say or do. It's only when you aren't being true to yourself, and you get caught, that you end up in trouble or you end up doing what's acceptable rather than what you really believe to be right."

Whatever it takes, refuse to be carried along by your work and its ongoing expectations. Like shown in the example above, when you create a rhythm of stepping back from your work and looking at it as an outsider would, you grant yourself the freedom to consider the ways in which you might be compromising in order to placate, or the areas in which you might be growing stagnant out of a fear of uncertainty. Your sense of self emerges in the space you grant to the process of reflection, assimilation, and redirection. When that space is squeezed out of your life, you may find yourself behaving reactively rather than from a deep sense of self-knowledge.

LETTING GO AND MOVING UP

There is a cycle of life and death baked into nature. We don't question it when the leaves shrivel and fall off trees in autumn, or when flowers die, or when fruit rots. It's just a part of how things work, and we know that the seeds that fall to the ground when these things happen perpetuate the cycle of life. However, we often don't allow for the same rhythmic cycles of life and death in our own lives, especially in our work. Once something is born, we feel the need to keep it going at all cost. We feel like to let something go is a sign of weakness or failure, or that it means we've not fulfilled our responsibility to the idea.

The need to squeeze every ounce of feasibility out of something can lead to stasis and eventually to block, frustration, and irrelevancy. Something that was once quite profound and resonant becomes a caricature of itself. Work that once "popped" is now blasé. By holding tightly to our assumptions about how things have to be, we often miss out on our potential.

Just like we do unquestionably with nature, we need to learn to embrace this important idea: sometimes something really good has to die so that something great can be born. It is the cycle of death and birth that fuels innovation, both in business and in our personal lives. It is also the central truth that drives the development of your authentic voice. You become stagnant when you hold on to good ideas long past their shelf life, or you refuse to disentangle yourself from something that once gave you a sense of identity and purpose simply because you are afraid of what will come next.

However, when you refuse to keep moving forward, you often begin to lose even the ground you've already taken. This is especially true in the process of developing your voice. It's easy to get stuck in a place of complacency once you've experienced a certain amount of success. You must remain humble enough to recognize when it's time to let go and move on.

There are strong urges and cultural forces that attempt to keep you in a place of perceived safety and prevent you from taking the kinds of risks necessary to develop and use your voice. They want you to preserve and protect what you've already done, even if it's at the expense of your body of work.

YOUR CONTRIBUTION IS A MOVIE, NOT A PHOTO

During a recent Q&A following a talk I gave, a gentleman arose to offer some thoughts about why it's so challenging to measure progress against the metrics that matter most to organizations. "The problem is," he said, "that when we measure, we like to capture what's going on right now, like a photo, but that's not really how organizations function." He went on to explain that the solution to better measuring progress and growth in key areas is to treat the organization like a movie, not a photo. Things are always progressing, regressing, trending in one way or another, and often behaving in unexpected ways. The only way to truly capture whether strategies are effective is to note the trend lines, not to attempt to capture metrics at some preappointed point in time.

The process of developing your voice is similar, in that on any given day you may not feel like you are making progress. It's only when you examine your accomplishments in context that you see that you truly are growing in all the meaningful ways. It is more about the pursuit than the accomplishment. In fact, it's often in the moments when you feel that you've finally hit upon something brilliant that you quickly recognize that a chasm has appeared between you and your next objective. The cognitive bias known as the Dunning-Kruger Effect illustrates that people at lower levels of skill tend to overestimate their abilities relative to others, but that the assessment flips with increased levels of competence. Those who are in reality more skilled than others tend to underestimate their own ability and assume that tasks that are easy for them are just as easy for others, even if they are acquired skills. For example, many writers consider their most celebrated work to be their least valuable artistically, and many leaders consider their valuable strategic insights to be obvious, or commonplace. This might lead to unwillingness to share ideas or give voice to concerns, if the assumption is that others must surely hold them as well. It can also—at times—lead to a destructive form of creative block if allowed to fester.

When everything seems obvious, nothing seems noteworthy or insight inducing. The key to overcoming this dynamic is to consistently put your work into the world as a matter of discipline. You have to get in the mix if you want to keep growing. Act now, and be patient for the results.

YOUR AUTHENTIC VOICE IS A GIFT THAT RETURNS TO YOU

Which comes first, the fruits of your talent or the willingness to generously and selflessly share it with others?

According to Lewis Hyde, author of *The Gift*, it's a virtuous cycle. The creative gift you've been given is not to use for your own purposes, it's to be given away to others, who will carry on the cycle of gift giving that will eventually return to you.

In the "cult of celebrity" that we've created, the desire for attention often trumps the desire to create and contribute value. If something has fewer likes, views, or shares, then it's deemed less valuable than something with viral appeal. As such, many people have taken to shape-shifting according to whatever will lend more social credibility. However, as Hyde says, celebrity should never be confused with essence.

As you consider the gift that you have to offer—the expression that is uniquely yours, and yours alone to give away—consider this: the impact of a gift given away in freedom is vast, while a gift spent on the giver quickly fades.

Your authentic voice is a gift. How will you offer it to others today through your work?

Answering that question is your life's mission.

ACKNOWLEDGMENTS

The real gift of writing is that it's an opportunity for your own thoughts and biases to be reshaped by your research, or by the voices of those you encounter along the way. I'm indebted to everyone who helped me find my voice in the midst of this project, and I'm grateful to those who allowed me to interview them, or who had little side conversations along the way to help me process my thoughts.

Thank you to my amazing editor, Emily Angell, for being a trusted voice, and to everyone at Portfolio who touched this book in some way, including Adrian Zackheim, Will Weisser, Margot Stamas, Jesse Maeshiro, and Kary Perez.

I'm grateful to my hard-working literary agent, Melissa Sarver-White, who continues to help me find a platform for my ideas. Also, many thanks to Tom Neilssen, Les Tuerk, Michele DiLisio, and the entire team at BrightSight Group for keeping me in front of audiences with whom I can share my voice.

Of course, no book is written without the support of the people closest to you. Rachel, thank you for the freedom and for always being my most valuable first reader. Ethan, Owen, and Ava, thank you for all of the little ways you surprise and delight me each day.

NOTES AND SELECTED FURTHER READING

Some of the ideas and thoughts in this book originally appeared on ToddHenry.com or AccidentalCreative.com. For more resources related to developing your voice, visit ToddHenry.com/louderthanwords.

I also produce a weekly podcast called The Accidental Creative, which can be found at AccidentalCreative.com.

CHAPTER TWO

The article on Elvis Presley at twenty-one, entitled "The First of Elvis," appeared in the January 2010 issue of *Vanity Fair* and was written by Bob Colacello, with photos by Al Wertheimer.

I heard Jia Jiang's talk at the World Domination Summit in Portland, Oregon. He later compiled his experiences into a 2015 book entitled *Rejection Proof*.

Richard Hytner was interviewed by me. He also wrote a book about his experiences called *Consiglieri: Leading from the Shadows*.

Status Anxiety by Alain de Botton is an excellent exploration of the problems and pressures associated with status seeking.

CHAPTER THREE

The 2009 Ira Glass interview on creativity and storytelling can be found at http://www.youtube.com/watch?v=BI23U7U2aUY.

The Rise by Sarah Lewis is a wonderful examination of the creative process, and the role of play and failure in innovation.

Joshua Foer discusses the OK Plateau in his book *Moonwalking with Einstein*.

The June 2012 Neil Peart interview on *RollingStone.com* was entitled "Q&A: Neil Peart on Rush's New LP and Being a 'Bleeding Heart Libertarian.'"

Mastery by Robert Greene examines how brilliant contributors become masters of their craft.

On Writing by Stephen King is the best book on writing that I've ever read.

The Steve Earle quote was from an interview with Grammy.com about his admiration of Woody Guthrie. The article can be found at http://www .grammy.com/news/steve-earle-talks-woody-guthrie-and-the-art-of -songwriting.

Steering the Craft by Ursula K. Le Guin is an excellent book of advice for writers.

Creativity by Mihaly Csikszentmihalyi remains one of my favorite explorations of the creative process, as he studies its practice through the lenses of multiple domains of expertise.

Peter Sims wrote a book called *Little Bets*, which discussed the need to take small chances with your work every day.

Jon Acuff's quote is from his book *Start*.

CHAPTER FOUR

Jocelyn Glei's story was from an interview with the author.

The Element by Ken Robinson explains how various people found their area of contribution.

The information on Edward Bernays is from his book *Propaganda*.

The Steve Jobs "creativity is just connecting things" quote is from a 1996 interview with *WIRED* magazine. It can be found at http://archive.wired.com /wired/archive/4.02/jobs_pr.html.

Steven Johnson's spark file insights can be found at https://medium.com/the-writers-room/the-spark-file-8d6e7df7ae58.

Frank Lloyd Wright's principles for his apprentices can be found in *Frank Lloyd Wright: An Autobiography.*

Amos Heller's story was from an interview with the author.

Z-Trip's story was from an interview with the author.

CHAPTER FIVE

Seth Goldman's story was from an interview with the author, with additional insights from his book *Mission in a Bottle.*

Seth Godin's talk was at the 99U conference, and can be viewed at http://99u.com/videos/35027/seth-godin-keep-making-a-ruckus.

Jimi Hendrix opened for The Monkees in the summer of 1967. One article describing the phenomenon can be found at http://www.history.com/this -day-in-history/jimi-hendrix-drops-out-as-opening-act-for-the-monkees.

More on the Hendrix/Monkees debacle, including cited quotes from the participants, is at http://www.snopes.com/music/artists/hendrix.asp.

The Empathic Civilization by Jeremy Rifkin explores emerging social dynamics and the need for global empathy to solve larger problems.

The LL Cool J concert in Waterville, Maine, can be seen at https://www .youtube.com/watch?v=1TqQ0rLY-Qo.

Jerry Haselmayer and Geoff Zoeckler were interviewed individually by the author.

The study of the truth campaign can be found at http://www.ncbi.nlm.nih .gov/pmc/articles/PMC1447480/.

Jeremy Pryor of Epipheo was interviewed by the author.

CHAPTER SIX

Malcolm Gladwell's book *Outliers* examines how extremely accomplished performers accomplished mastery.

Edgar Sandoval and Judy John, of the #LikeAGirl campaign, were interviewed by the author.

CHAPTER SEVEN

The Artist's Way by Julia Cameron offers an excellent program for anyone wishing to reclaim their creative voice and artistic spirit.

Accidental Genius by Mark Levy is by far the best how-to resource for free writing.

Essentialism by Greg McKeown offers strategies for simplifying life and work.

Cal Newport's writing on deep work can be found on his Web site, CalNewport.com, and in his excellent book *So Good They Can't Ignore You.*

CHAPTER NINE

Donald Knuth's quote on premature optimization, in full, is "We *should* forget about small efficiencies, say about 97% of the time: premature optimization is the root of all evil. Yet we should not pass up our opportunities in that critical 3%." It appeared in a paper entitled "Structured Programming with go to Statements."

Kevin Kelly's excellent interview on the Tim Ferriss podcast can be heard at http://fourhourworkweek.com/2014/08/29/kevin-kelly/.

riCardo Crespo was interviewed by the author.

The Gift by Lewis Hyde is a beautiful and classic book about the creative act, gift giving, and generosity.

INDEX

Index

Index

Index

Index

Index

Index